Wallpaper

in the Collection
of the
Cooper-Hewitt
Museum

The Smithsonian
Institution's
National Museum
of Design

Foreword

From its beginnings to recent pop art and super-graphic manifestations, wallpaper has offered a fascinating reflection of styles and fluctuating taste in the broader world of decorative arts. One of the largest and most comprehensive collections of wallpaper in the world has been assembled by the Cooper-Hewitt Museum.

Over 6,000 catalogued items gathered over fourscore years include genuine leather wallcoverings tooled by 17th century artisans in Flanders, Oriental hand painted papers and canvas, fine American, English, French, and other European printed papers, and composition and vinyl coverings. Salesmen's sample books, stencils, screens, block, and rollers are all part of the collection.

The Wallpaper Department of the Cooper-Hewitt provides a centralized research facility for architectural historians, restorationists, students, designers, and others who are interested in studying the development of wallpaper design internationally. The Department has been strongly supported by the trade. This publication was made possible through the kindness of Brunschwig & Fils, Inc.—longtime friends of the Museum.

Lisa Taylor
Director

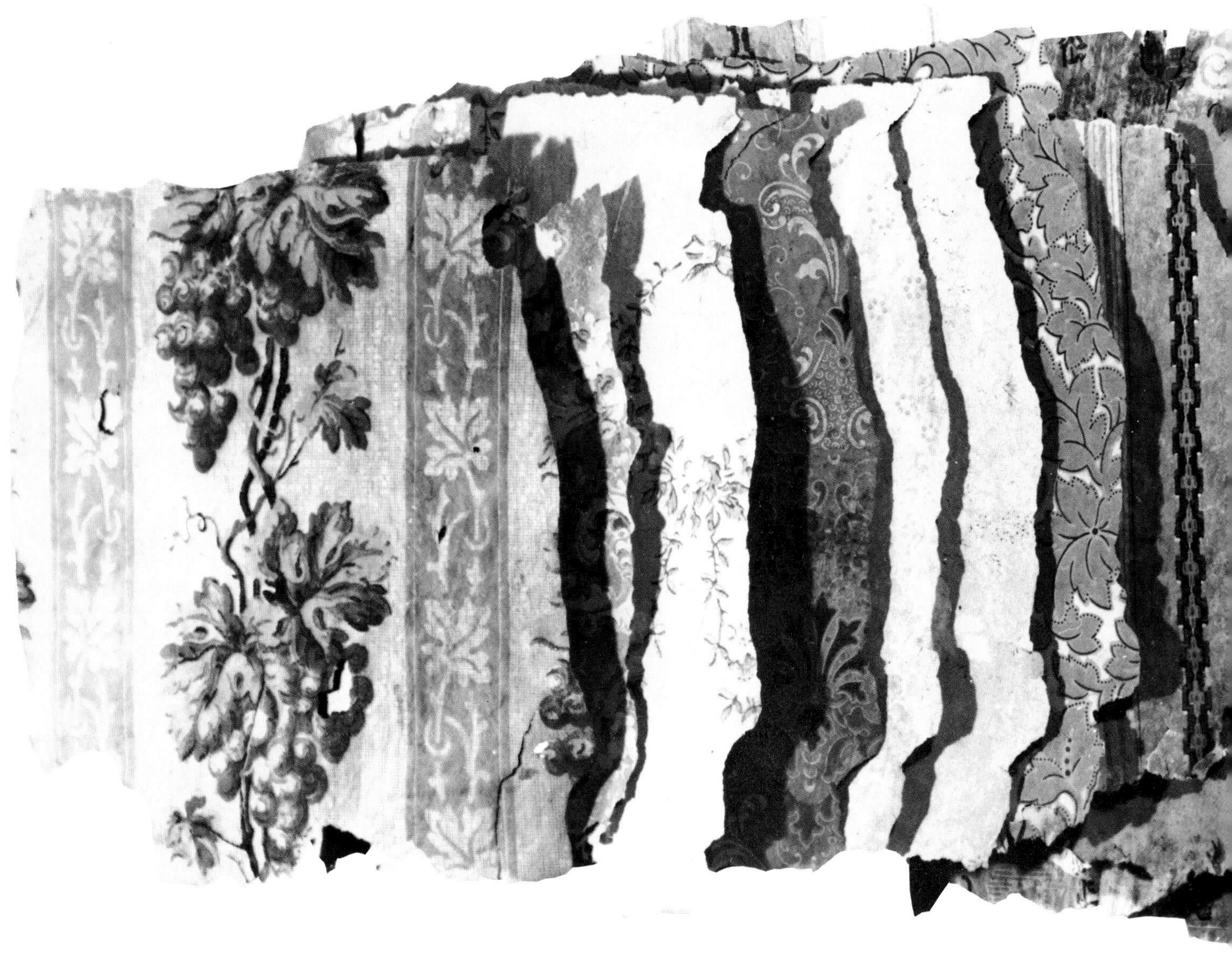

Thirteen layers of wallpaper from one wall of the Nathan Beers House, Fairfield, Connecticut

The earliest pattern, shown on the far right, is a rainbow paper of the 1820s, the colors of the patterned areas blending from yellow through green to blue. The grape pattern on the far left is machine-printed in maroon and green over beige. It dates from the turn of the twentieth century.

The gift of Edith L. R. Fisher, 1960-211-1

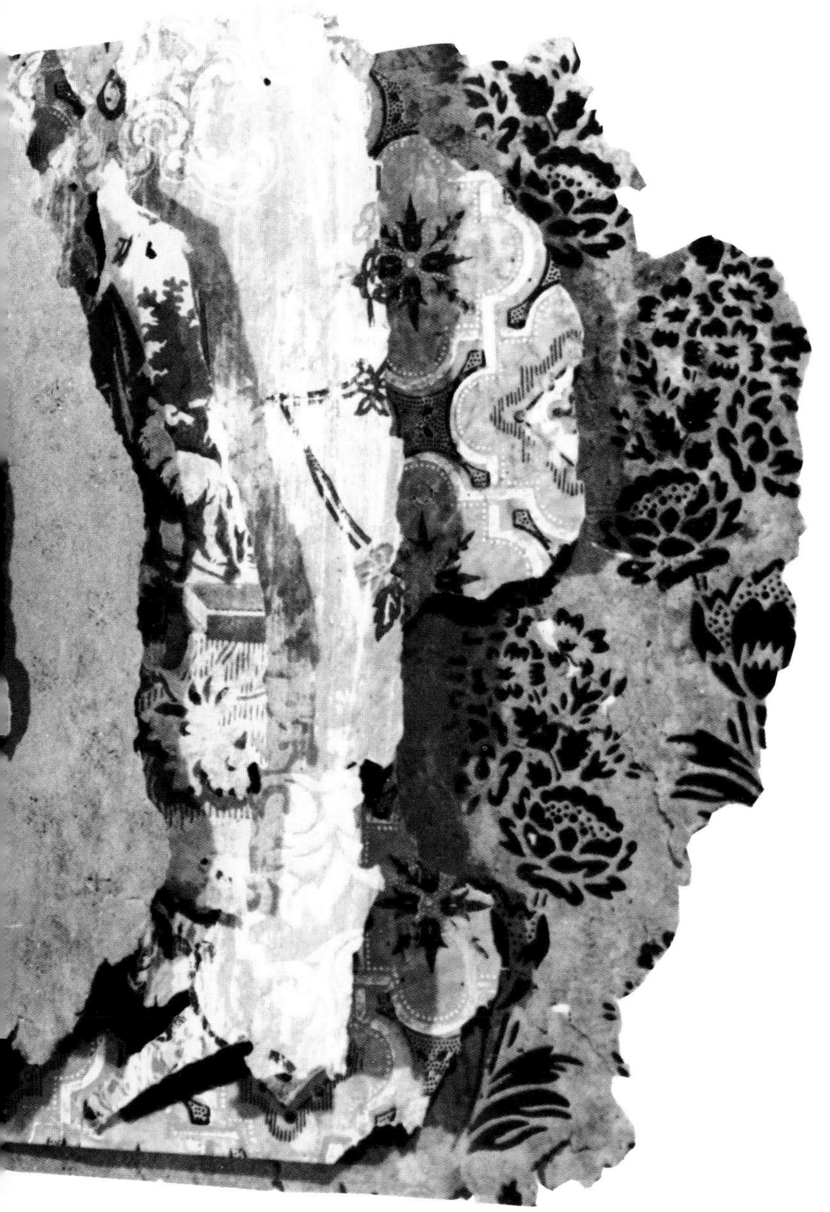

"It's the wallpaper or me—one of us has to go" Oscar Wilde quipped as he lay dying in a Parisian hotel in 1900—or so a friend reported. *The Yellow Wallpaper* is the title of the best work of fiction by Charlotte Perkin's Gilman, America's most perceptive feminist theoretician of the nineteenth century. It was published in 1892. By the late nineteenth century, wallpaper, which had made its first appearances in the West during the sixteenth century, was to be found in nearly every house. And such references attest to the fact that it was making its impression on a great many minds as well. Even the writers of scientific works brought wallpaper into their textbooks. Finding that wallpaper designs offered convenient and familiar examples of structural principles, some authors included illustrations of wallpapers in introductory discussions of crystal symmetry and space filling.

Late nineteenth century realistic novels are filled with scenes that take place in rooms in which wallpaper is noted. As a literary motif, wallpaper usually figures as a sign of falseness, of shallow pretension, of sham in late nineteenth century writings. And in Charlotte Perkin's Gilman's chilling *The Yellow Wallpaper* it figures as a living presence. Gilman traces stages in the growth of derangement within the mind of a "neurasthenic" house wife oppressed by her "dear John," a husband whose ministrations serve only to frustrate her and to intensify her pain. Gilman reveals changes in the victim's grip on reality by describing her shifting perceptions of the pattern on the walls, a pattern which entraps a shadowy presence, an image of herself. In a final act of lucid madness, she frees that shadow-self by ripping the paper off the walls.

While a great many Americans were contented and calm within their patterned walls, Oscar Wilde's implication that the wallpaper was killing him, and Gilman's depiction of a character moved to physically attack such harmless-seeming stuff, are resonant of a general reaction against the overuse of pattern that was setting in as the turn of the century approached. By this time, countless writers had successfully promoted the use of multiple patterns and borders. Wallpaper appeared in newspaper articles, in lengthy pieces in popular magazines as well as in more profound publications, and in long chapters in books on decorating. Manufacturers were printing ever-increasing quantities of paper, which they often described in terms of the number of times their annual production could circle the earth. These manufacturers enlisted the talents of major artists and architects to design patterns for their printing machines. Their celebrated recruits included Louis C. Tiffany, Samuel Colman, and John Welborn Root in this country, William Burgess, E. W. Godwin, Walter Crane and many others in England.

In 1885 the California architects Newsom and Newsom declared in *Picturesque California Homes* that housepapering was a standard part of any contract for housebuilding and that "white walls unrelieved by pattern are relics of bar-

barism." But by the turn of the twentieth century, white walls were becoming symbols of incipient modernism, or alternatively, of a new fashion in interior decorating that revived preferences for finishing walls with light paint colors and architectural moldings in houses built in classical style. A generation of tastemakers that included characters as divergent as the decorator Elsie De Wolfe and the architect Frank Lloyd Wright banished what they perceived to have been the oppressive multiplicity of patterns familiar in the homes of their parents from the rooms of people concerned either with the principles of a new, indeed the "true," architecture, or with the chic and fashionable in home decorating.

After the late nineteenth century period when wallpaper design seems to have been of interest to everyone came a period when it was dimissed from the thinking of the avante-garde and the stylish. During the early twentieth century manufacturers continued to print wallpaper patterns in ever-increasing quantities and the decorating trade continued to use it consistently, but wallpaper suffered a serious decline in status. Recovery from that decline did not gain momentum before the 1970s. Many who were influenced by the architectural theories of the modern movement and by the winds of fashion that wafted after the close of World War I branded wallpaper as passé. They were not shaken in that conviction until Post-Modernists of the 1970s began to substitute a variety of decorative finishes for the "honest" white wall of the Modernists. As the Post-Modernists have

turned to examples of historic architecture, especially to monuments in a variety of classical styles, for many of their recently-built houses, so they find they can learn a great deal about the ornamenting of walls from early patterns. And among their ranks a newly enthusiastic audience for the collection of wallpapers at the Cooper-Hewitt Museum can be anticipated.

This new audience will join long-existing and usually specialized audiences who constitute users of this archive, the finest and most comprehensive collection of wallpaper in America, and one of the best in the world. Sarah and Eleanor Hewitt, founders of what was originally the Cooper-Union Museum, began to collect wallpaper early in this century. French wallpapers of the late eighteenth and early nineteenth centuries formed the bulk of their collection. This nucleus acted as a magnet that has attracted gifts to the Museum ranging from members of the wallpaper industry to homeowners who, in the process of steaming off old papers, have discovered early specimens.

Architectural preservationists, restorers, and curators often come across wallpapers pasted one atop another in odd nooks and crannies of the houses in their care. Probing like archaeologists through the shallow layers of time papered on the vertical surface of a wall, it is not rare to find a series like that of thirteen layers illustrated as the frontispiece of this handbook. By comparison with specimens in the encyclopedic collection at the Museum, the discoverers of old papers can often date and identify what they have found and can learn to recognize wallpaper styles appropriate to their restorations.

The grandiosity of wallpaper patterns is often surprising. Even in simple houses, evidence of the use of elaborate nineteenth-century designs and of combinations of wallpaper elements often survives. In many houses, the series of patterns preserved on a given wall present somewhat dizzying varieties of approaches to the decoration of a wall. Because examples representing a wide spectrum of the theory and practice of wallpaper design are available at the Cooper-Hewitt, the collection proves especially useful to contemporary pattern designers. They find here wallcoverings dating from the seventeenth century to the present. The largest number are French and American, but many examples are included from other European countries and China. In this handbook some representative papers chosen from among the more than 6,000 catalogued samples, sets of papers, and samplebooks in the Cooper-Hewitt collection provide examples of the major techniques for adorning the surfaces of wallpapers: painting, flocking, wood-block printing by hand, roller printing by machine, and silk-screen printing.

In addition, the major approaches to embellishing blank walls are suggested. Although quite different one from another, during the past four centuries all have been simultaneously present, but each has fluctuated in fashionable preference. While wallpaper manufacturers and house decorators have devised ambitious wallpaper-ing schemes intended to dominate rooms, they have also created many others in which patterned papers are but subordinate elements within interiors. Some wallpapers are conceived as harmonious backgrounds for other interior decorations, or as minor elements within a more important architectural framework. Still others are designed merely as inconspicuous, perhaps textured, surfaces upon which to hang pictures, or as means of coloring and sealing the walls, or of hiding the cracks. The designers of other patterns modestly aspired to break the monotony of the flat plane of the wall-surface with stripes or spots, to entertain the eye with flower sprigs or with little pictures powdered across its expanses. More ambitious paper stainers (as wallpaper manufacturers were called in the 18th century) often created wallpapers to disguise walls, either by giving them surface coatings of what appear to be expensive materials—marble, exotic wood, leather, lustrous silk, or thick woven tapestry—or by covering them with illusionistic representations of scenes and objects that dislocate the surface. Some of these papers seem to pierce the wall so that it becomes a window opening on vistas receding into a far distance. Others supply fake elements of architectural or sculptural embellishment that appear to project from the wall, seeming to impinge on the actual space of the room. Decorators have long availed themselves of wallpaper's celebrated potential for visually enlarging, contracting, heightening or lowering the apparent dimensions of walls and ceilings.

The French reign as the triumphant exploiters of possibilities for fooling the eye with perspective drawing, atmospheric coloring, and skillful manipulation of shading in wallpaper. In the 1870s, Messrs. Desfossé et Karth, leading Parisian manufacturers, summed up a principle which had guided the industry in France for about a century: "Wallpaper being before all else an art of falsification, should never give the lie to its first destination."

In face of the long-standing success of French paper stainers in marketing wallpapers based on just principles, (see figures 8-11,17) it is doubtless no coincidence that, during the mid-nineteenth century, many of their less-successful English competitors embraced a set of design theories that discredited the French products. By 1850, English manufacturers were responding to the assertion, later summarized by Charles Locke Eastlake in *Hints on Household Taste* (1868), that

> "... common sense points to the fact that as a wall represents the flat surface of a solid material ... it should be decorated after a manner which will belie neither its flatness nor solidity. For this reason, all shaded ornament, and patterns, which by their arrangement of color give an appearance of relief, should be strictly avoided. Where natural forms are introduced, they should be treated in a conventional manner, i.e. drawn in pure outline, and filled in with flat color, never rounded."

During the second half of the nineteenth century, under the influence of this kind of theory, to which a heavy dose of pedantic

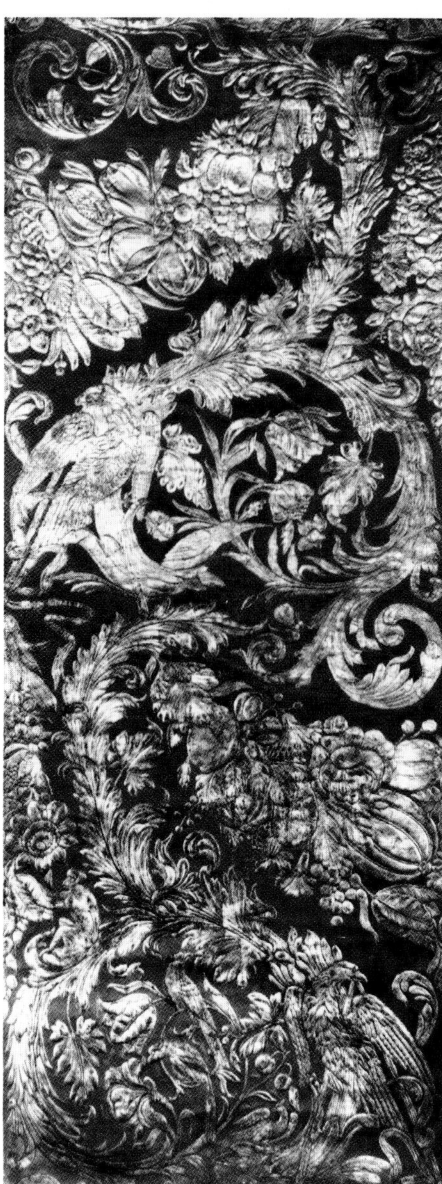

moralizing was appended, the English produced a quantity of self-consciously "flat patterns" devoid of shadows suggesting a third dimension. (See figure 22) Yet between the two extremes of illusionistic and self-consciously "flat" designs manufacturers continued, as they always had, to produce quantities of patterns in which they demonstrated little concern for consistent logical treatment of spatial effects and illusions. (See figures 5, 15, 17, 18) A scattering of realistic elements appearing to project in low relief from the surface of the paper might well be punctuated by "openings" that afforded a glimpse into a vignetted scene receding to a background deep in space, a scene illogically repeated countless times over the surface of a wall.

The examples illustrated in this booklet must be imagined within their larger contexts. These single elements, isolated repeats, or parts of suites were themselves only elements within architectural contexts or decorative schemes incorporating upholstery, curtains, and rugs that matched or contrasted with the papers both in color and in patterning. Seen in repeat, some of these wallpaper motifs formed stripes, diamond grids or other geometric configurations. All the repeating patterns, and many of the decorative wallpaper elements illustrated on these pages, would have been used in combination with wallpaper borders. Even the wallpaper pictures, and the great scenics shown here, were hung with wide borders at the top and wallpaper dados below the chair rail. Often wallpaper columns, pilasters, or patterned borders introduced vertical divisions to the wall.

People have long admired the gleam of gold in wall decorations, not only because its intrinsic value connotes great wealth: its light-reflecting qualities multiply the power of flickering flames. The irregularity of the relief on the tooled surfaces to which goldleaf is applied on leather (Figure 1) multiplies the faceting of light and adds to the lively movement as reflections bounced off the angles and curves of these surfaces. This seventeenth-century Flemish leather, a direct and close ancestor of wallpaper, is a tour-de-force of the kind executed by skilled workmen in Spain and Flanders for the walls of a few of the richest people. Two panels were required to make up a full repeat of this design: a complementary panel—a mirror image of the one shown here—would have completed the heavy swags of luscious golden fruit and foliage upon which great falcons perch over a blue background. The luxuriance of the materials is echoed in the Renaissance decorative vocabulary displayed here.

The low-relief projection in leathers of this type was copied not only in late nineteenth-century imitations of leather (Figure 22) but also throughout the eighteenth and nineteenth centuries. Paper stainers skillfully shaded printed forms on flat surfaces to produce a cheaper substitute for this kind of wallcovering. Such early papers were embellished with gold and

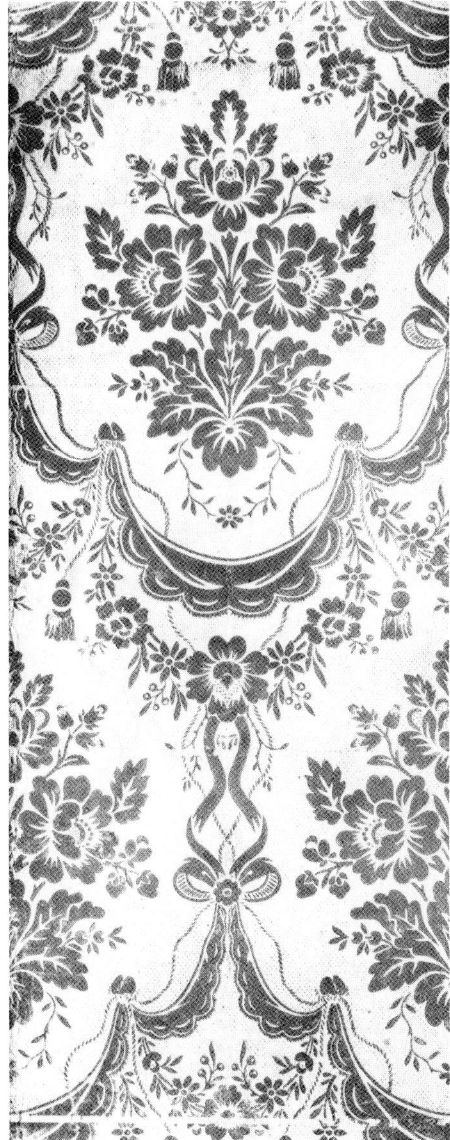

with other light-reflecting materials including powdered mica or isinglas.

While a select few used expensive leathers and textiles on their walls, some early sixteenth-century Europeans were beginning to paste and tack up papers printed with images and decorative patterning. The use of paper hangings in the West as early as 1509 is documented by a paper found on beams in a house in Cambridge, printed by a book printer of York, England. Papers to be hung on walls were printed from woodblocks along with end papers for books, papers for lining boxes and trunks, and playing cards. By the sixteenth century French craftsmen called *dominotiers* enjoyed some renown for these products. Their name was perhaps derived from *dominus,* an association appropriate because members of their guild also produced religious images.

In the mid-eighteenth century, a French *dominotier* used woodblocks to print in black ink the outlines of a single sheet of patterning shown in *figure 2.* Then he brushed on watercolor washes probably with the aid of stencils. Regulations imposed at the instigation of rival guilds restricted the *dominotiers* to printing on such single sheets, but patterns like this, in which the design continues beyond the confines of a single sheet, not only appear to be conceived as appropriate for walls: they have also been found pasted and tacked on them.

Domino papers were made by craftsmen whose primary concern for decorative embellishment had been limited to the small surfaces of book covers and box interiors. Craftsmen accustomed to design and produce textiles that draped more expansive surfaces of walls and windows also influenced the design of paper hangings. Paper stainers preempted not only large quantities of designs and craft techniques from the textile industry, but they also took craftsmen, particularly the woodblock carvers and printers. The textile trades had developed cheaper substitutes for the most expensive hangings at an early date. For instance, to imitate luxurious cut velvets and woolen piles, they had learned to make flocking—powdered cuttings and shavings of wool or silk—and to fix flocking on the surfaces of textiles, including canvas, with adhesives. English and German flocked canvas wall hangings of the seventeenth century are represented in the Cooper-Hewitt collections. By the seventeenth century, those flocked canvas wallhangings were supplemented by flocked papers. The English became masters in this technique.

Before decorating such papers they glued together, or "joined," individual sheets to form rolls twelve feet long. Then workmen brushed into the joined sheets a coating—"a ground"—of varnish color. Adhesive was applied to the areas to be flocked, either by painting it on or by block-printing patterns of glue over the colored paper surface. Finally, they distributed the finely-powdered flocking, which would stick only to the areas prepared with the still-wet adhesive.

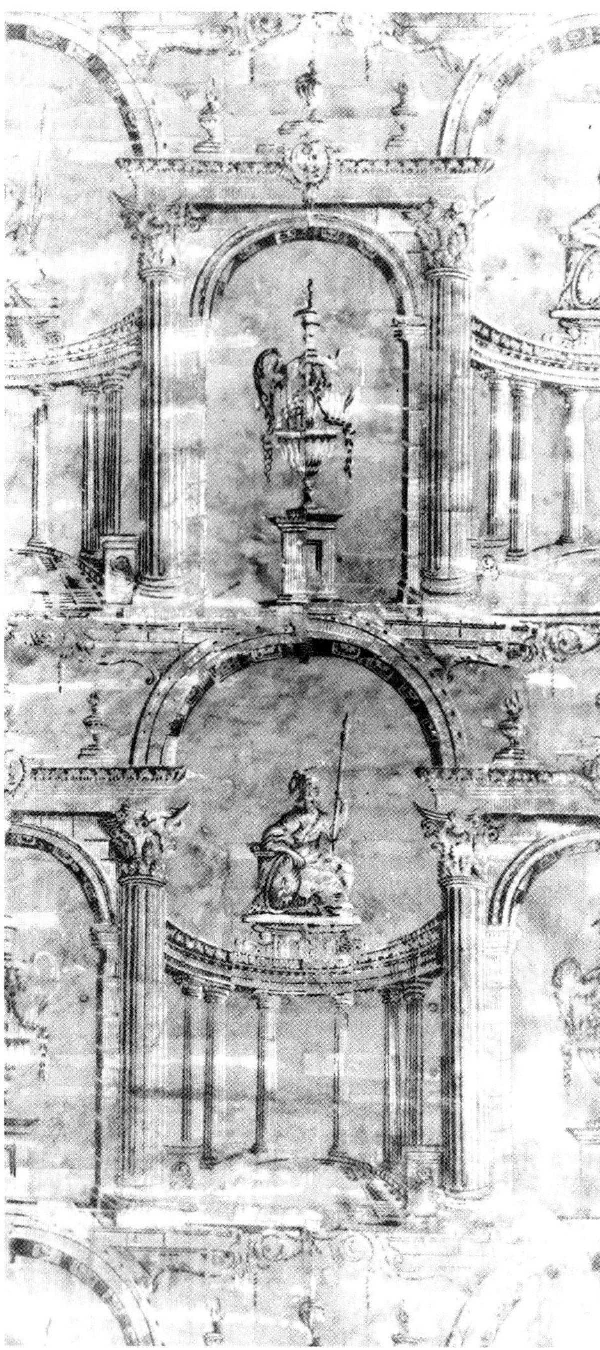

By the eighteenth century the English were well-advanced in the craft. The paper shown in figure 3 imitates a large-scale luxurious silk damask pattern. The matte effect of the darker flocking contrasts with the shiny golden yellow of the varnished background, imitating the contrasts achieved by varying the weaves in damasks. Wallpaper makers borrowed floral motifs from the repertory of textile weavers who flattened and simplified the forms, eliminating shaded effects of modeling and relief.

If textiles provided the prototypes for the largest numbers of wallpapers, architectural ornament furnished a great many as well. During the eighteenth century, the French and English alike printed full scale eye-fooling elements of interior trim, paper panels for dados intended to look like wainscoting and like moldings for chair rail and cornice, rosettes to look like plaster ceiling centers, borders simulating carved and plaster-work frames and other elements imitating columns and pilasters.

Although eighteenth-century craftsmen printed conservative and purely classical versions of pilasters like the later and more elaborate example of figure 17, they also took architectural motifs, reduced their scale, and showed them in repeat (Figure 4). During the 1790s, Zecheriah Mills, a paper stainer of Hartford, Connecticut, block-printed this pattern in exact, though reversed, duplication of an English paper. An example of its English prototype, found in a house in Old Saybrook, Connecticut, is also in the collections of the Cooper-Hewitt. The American reversal of the En-

Figure 4
"Domino" paper, a single ungrounded sheet with
    patterning for which the outlines are wood-block
    printed in ink, and the colors filled in as stencilled
    washes
France; mid-eighteenth century
14¼ inches wide; black outlines, yellow, red, and
    blue washes
The gift of Eleanor and Sarah Hewitt, 1928-2-77

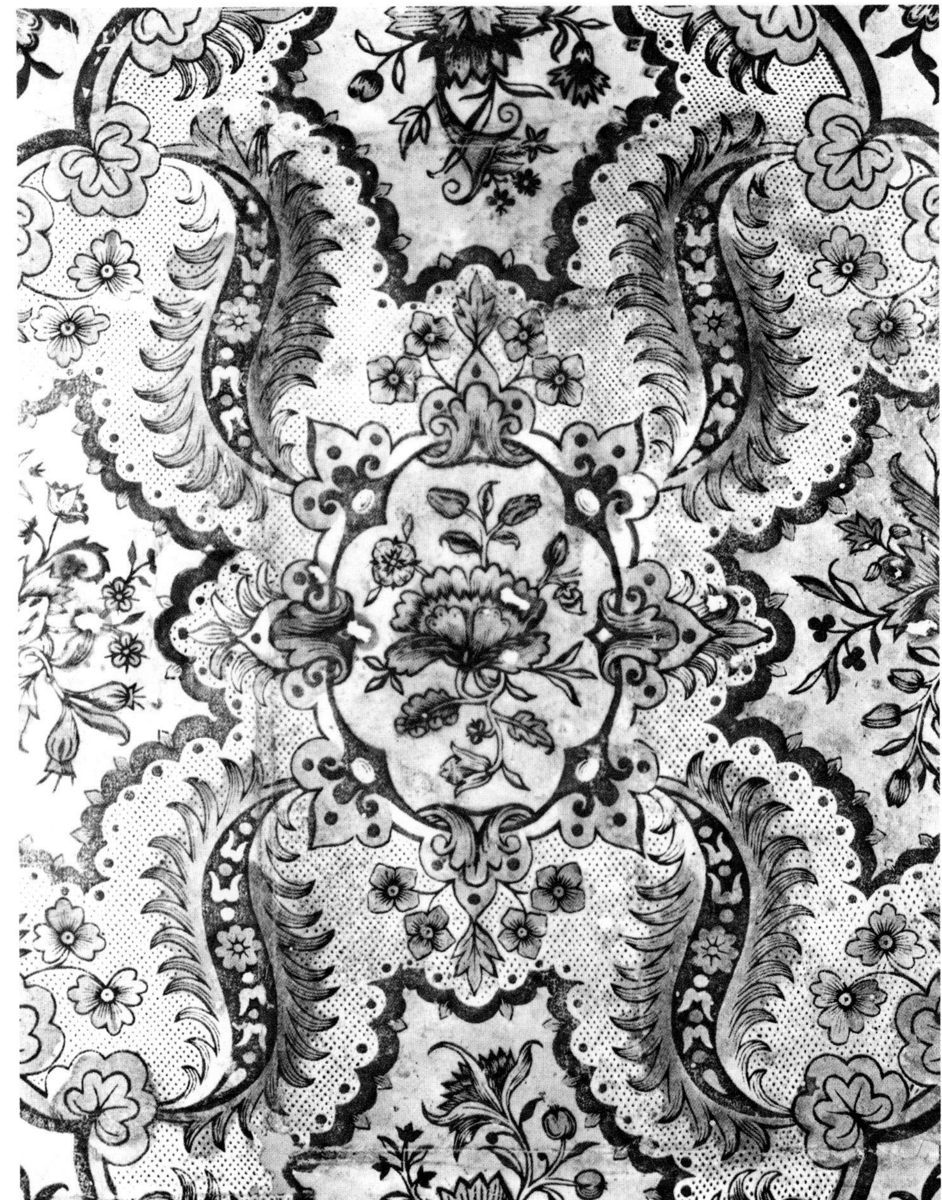

glish pattern is the printed result of drawing
from the original directly onto the face of
the printing block. The eighteenth-century
English fondness for shades of gray in
wallpapers is reflected in the English original, while Mills enhanced his version of it
with a blue background.

With the Revolution only two decades
behind him, it is surprising that an American would have incorporated the politically
resonant figure of Britannia into his wallpaper pattern, but not at all surprising that
he would have reproduced the format and
stylistic characteristics of a familiar and
still-admired English wallpaper style:
Other American craftsmen continued to
emulate English models in architecture and
furnishing.

American paper stainers relied almost
exclusively on English styles throughout
the Colonial period until French styles
began to dominate the American wallpaper
market during the 1790s. The sombre pal-
ettes of the English and English-inspired
patterns appear dull in comparison to the
dazzling array of distemper colors in these
new French wallpapers.

French paper stainers, led by Jean
Papillon (1661–1723) and by his son,
Jean-Michel Papillon (1698–1776) refined
English block-printing techniques. Their
advances were carried further by Jean-
Baptiste Réveillon (active 1765–89).
Réveillon's paper staining establishment
at the "Folie Titon", a mansion in the
Faubourg St. Antoine, the paper-staining
center of Paris, had become a veritable fac-
tory, employing 300 when its international

fame was enhanced in 1783: In that year, the grounds of the factory served as the site for the first balloon ascension by the Montgolfier Brothers. In 1784, Louis XVI named Réveillon's establishment a "Royal Manufactory." During the French Revolution, Réveillon fled to England, and in 1791, he turned his factory over to Jacquemart et Bénard.

The factory's most distinctive contribution was the high-style arabesque panel (Figure 5). It was ultimately based on classical sources, but the best-known arabesques were the painted wall decorations executed by Raphael at the Vatican. They are characterized by central vertical stems from which all manner of natural and fantastic growth springs into graceful curves. These are adorned with birds, beasts, and insects and frequently interrupted by plaques, roundels, architectural elements and a wide variety of other fanciful devices. In Réveillon's elegant wallpaper arabesques, dozens of blocks were used to print a brilliant but subtle array of colors, most frequently over pastel blue grounds. A distinctive combination of pastel shades with touches of intense pure colors, especially orange, appears in the products of Réveillon's factory. The slender graceful forms shimmer on the wall in a realm of shallow space, only ambiguously suggested by the solid ground color behind them. At reduced scale, motifs appropriated from arabesque panels were incorporated in repeating patterns that featured neo-classical elements —urns, tripods, relief panels, and *tempietti*. And in examples that deviated playfully

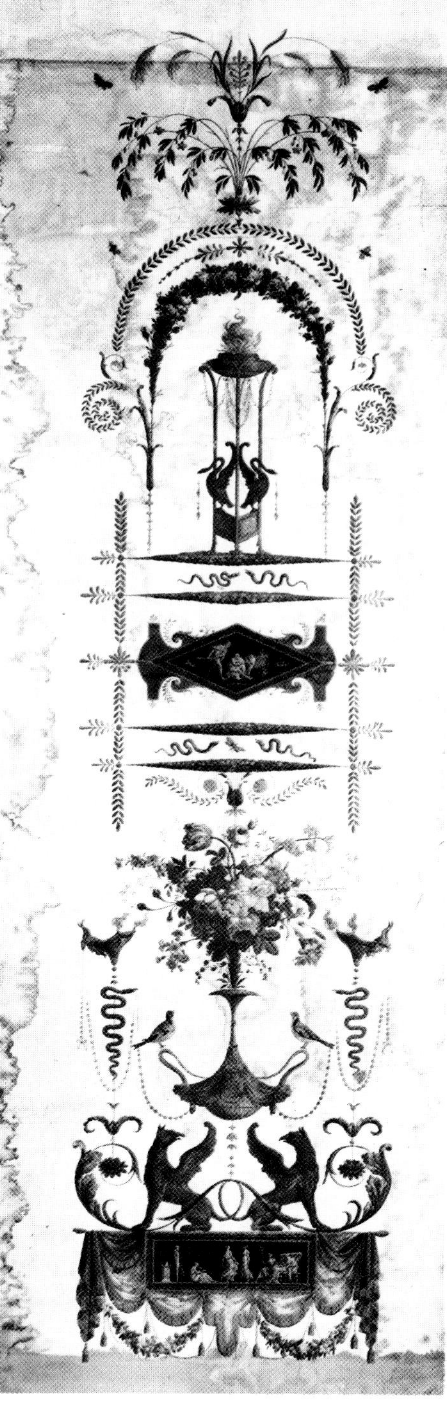

from the classical models, chinoiserie motifs were sometimes introduced with an eye toward pleasing all tastes.

Beginning in the early seventeenth century, when ships of the Dutch East India Company first brought quantities of Chinese goods to the West, the rich and powerful developed a taste for Oriental arts. Among these, painted, rather than printed, papers were greatly admired (Figure 6). Based on ancient Chinese paintings on scrolls, such papers were always expensive commodities hung only in the homes of the rich; by the eighteenth century they had achieved the status of the most desirable of wall coverings. Westerners were fascinated by the elegantly rendered motifs: flowering trees bedecked with exotic birds and insects like this example, or landscapes in which details of tea cultivation, pottery making, the theater, or the activities of daily life in a rural village were detailed in vignettes. The scenes were stacked one above another so that events in the far distance were brought up close for inspection.

Chinese export wallpapers influenced Western production of wallpaper during the eighteenth century by setting high standards for materials, clarity and brightness of colors, and fastidiousness of rendered detail. They inspired imitations, both painted versions as close to originals as Western skills could achieve, and cheaper printed imitations. They also served as sources for motifs which were often incorporated in repeating patterns of decidedly Western format. Whimsical Chinese figures often found their way into Gothic arches

13

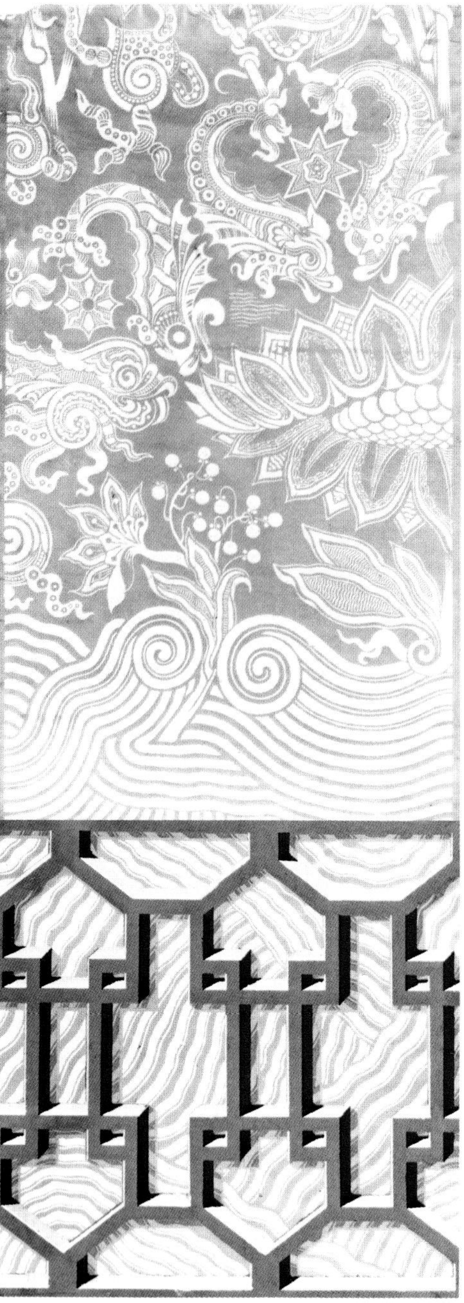

and classical garden buildings in wallpapers printed by French, English, and American craftsmen.

The English wallpapers illustrated as figure 7 suggest another way in which Chinese designs were westernized. Here flattened and abstracted motifs, reminiscent of those embroidered on the silk ceremonial robes of Chinese nobility, have been worked into sophisticated two-dimensional patterns. Duplicate patterns, differently colored, were used during the 1820s in the bedroom of the Prince Regent in his Royal Pavillion at Brighton. The samples pictured are two of the 12 wallpapers from the future king's oriental fantasy house remodeled by the architect John Nash (1752–1835) and decorated by Frederick Crace (1779–1859) during the 1820s. The wallpapers at Cooper-Hewitt are colorful supplements to the museum's collection of Crace's original drawings for the decorations.

While such adaptations of Chinese motifs as those used at Brighton fluctuated in popularity during the nineteenth century, the Chinese flowering tree papers retained a solid if sometimes minor place in the wallpaper trade which has extended even to the present day. They established a taste for large-scale, non-repeating scenes covering entire walls from chair-rail to ceiling with colorful decoration. Chinese landscapes whetted Western appetites for the narrative and anecdotal qualities which wallcoverings could add to interior decoration. Around 1800 French wallpaper man-

ufacturers began to block print landscape
views for customers who could not afford
the painted Chinese versions, or who preferred themes derived from more familiar
Western sources (Figure 9).

Evaluated simply as examples of a
printing technique, these scenic papers
rank as *tours de force* of color printing in
multiple on a scale never before attempted.
Some full sets covered wall spaces 10 feet
high with 50 horizontal feet of non-
repeating views. Thousands of individu-
ally-carved woodblocks and hundreds of
colors were often used to print a single
scenic paper. When regarded in context,
covering all the walls of a room from chair
rail to ceiling with continuous, non-
repeating scenes rendered in convincing
perspective, these papers emerge as spec-
tacular and bold popularizations of the
painterly arts of illusion, piercing the wall
surface and opening up a room to all out-
doors. Householders of the prosperous
upper middle classes could afford these
convincing approximations of the art of
skilled painters. Scenic papers were printed
in large numbers, and marketed in whole-
sale quantities all over the world. The
Zuber factory in Alsace, only one of eight
or ten major producers of landscape papers, shipped its products to 100 dealers in
the United States during the 1820s and 30s,
as well as to buyers in India, Hong Kong, all
the great cities on the European continent,
Russia, Britain, and South America.

The subject matter of these papers was
various: landscapes showing country and

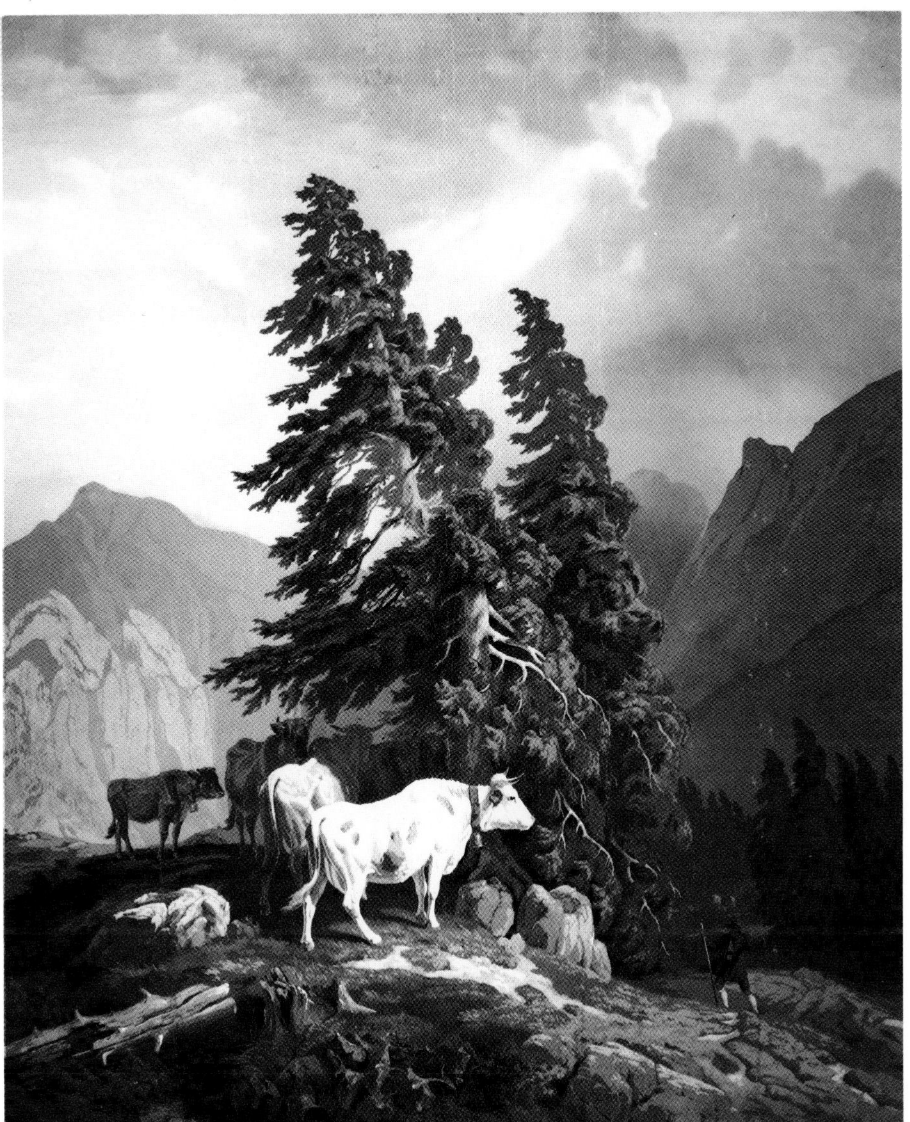

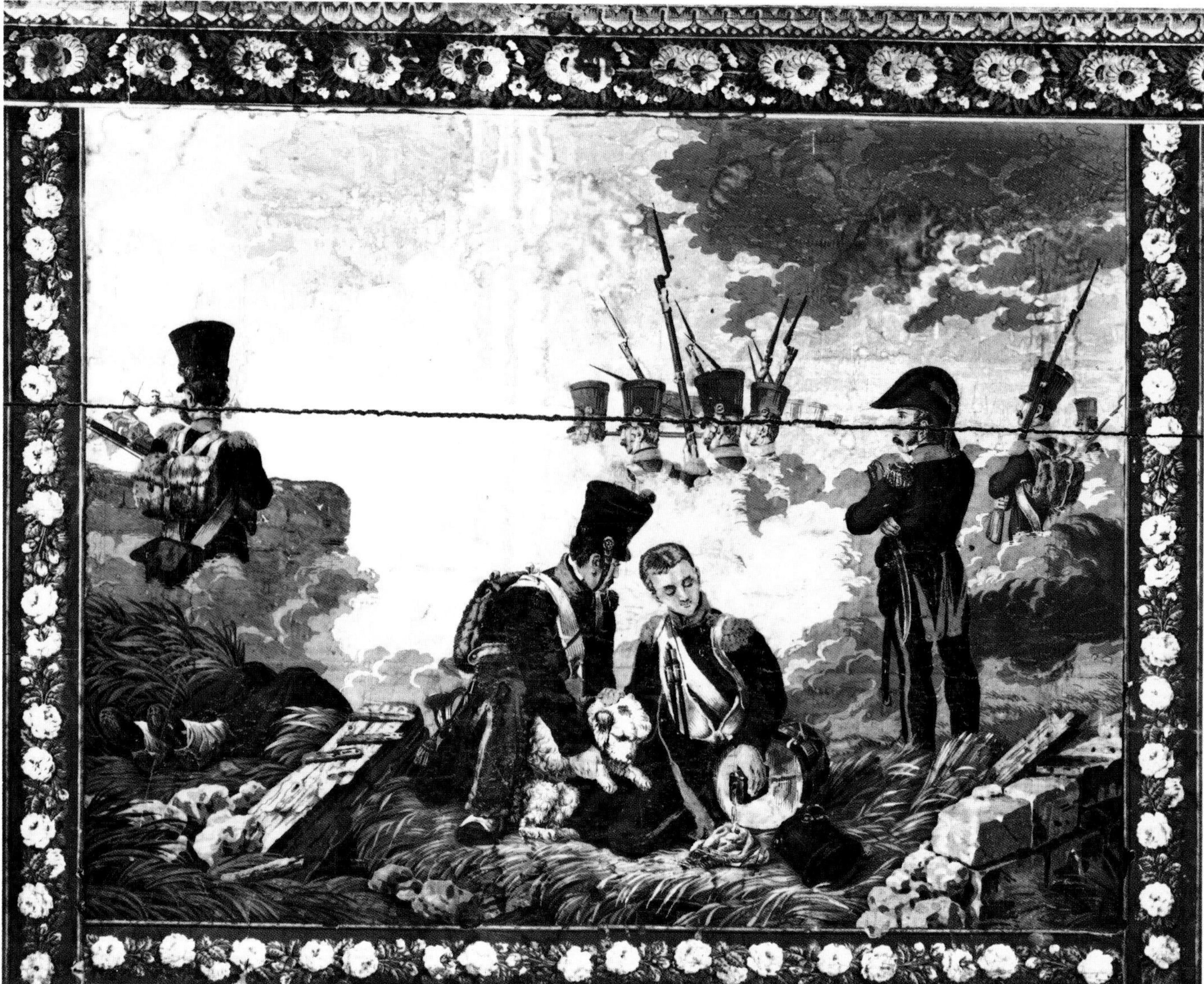

Figure 9

"Le Chien du Regiment," block-printed wallpaper pic-
ture mounted on a wooden fire board and framed
with wallpaper borders
Rixheim, Alsace, France; printed by Zuber c. 1815-45
49½ inches wide, multicolored
This fireboard was part of the furnishings of Ringwood
Manor, the New Jersey home of the donor
The gift of Mrs. A. S. Hewitt, 1907-15-4

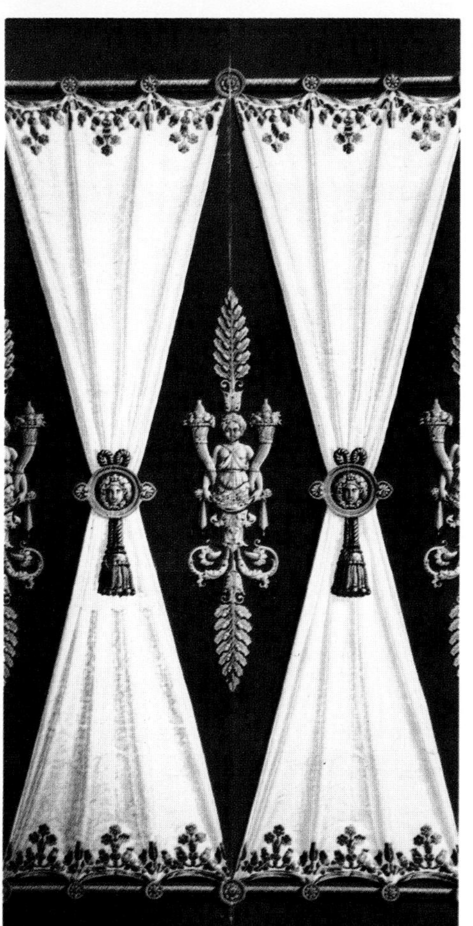

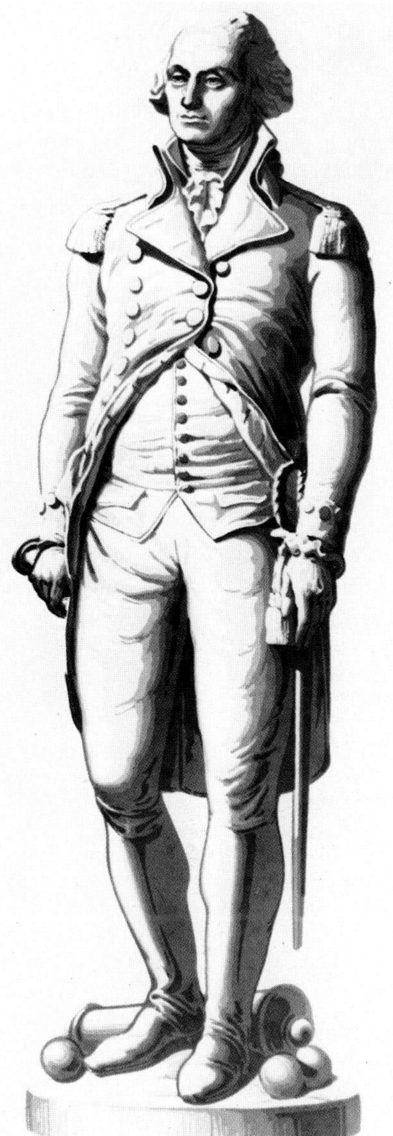

city, mountains and riversides, gardens and busy harbors. The scenes they depicted were set in Europe as well as in more exotic regions — the banks of the Bosporus, jungles in India, and palaces in China. Some of the scenic papers showed historical events — Captain Cook's adventures in the South Pacific; the early nineteenth century Greek war for independence; and Napoleon's battles; others illustrated classical myths and popular romantic novels.

The French manufacturers who block-printed the wall-sized "long-strip-landscapes", as nineteenth-century advertisements sometimes described them, used their facilities to print easle-sized pictures as well. In the one shown as figure 9, the plight of the regiment's dog, whose wounds are being dressed even in the midst of battle, was calculated to pluck the heartstrings of any sentimentalist. This wallpaper picture has been "framed" with wallpaper borders and mounted on a wooden board, cut to a size to fill a fireplace opening when no fire was burning. In addition to their use as fireboards, wallpaper pictures of this general size were also popular through most of the nineteenth century as overdoor and overmantle decorations, indeed as cheap pictures to hang on the wall.

If the use of wallpaper pictures during the early nineteenth-century exploited the illusionistic possibilities of piercing the surfaces of walls, the use of a great many equally illusionistic and realistic imitations of architectural ornaments and pseudo-drapery demonstrated the ways non-existent objects might be made to appear to project from the walls. Decorators not only hung representations of elaborate draperies (Figure 10), but also swagged, festooned, tasseled, bejeweled and befeathered drapery borders and friezes. Most often these were hung at cornice level, even when elaborate landscape papers filled the wall below.

French manufacturers also used their woodblocks to depict sculptured figures. George Washington as shown in figure 11 is one of the four heroes of the American Revolution included in the set clearly targeted for a specific export market. Classical statues were the most popular. The French paper stainers also made wallpaper plinths on which to display these statues, and produced other trimmings for these works of art. American dealers and importers sometimes advertised wallpaper statues "with or without niches."

While the French specialized in such *trompe l'oeil* elaborations of the block-printer's art throughout the nineteenth century, they and their international competitors printed patterns intended to reside more statically within the viewer's perception of the wall surface. The Austrian designers of the wall decorations illustrated in figure 12 were clearly less concerned with questions of illusion, and more concerned with the problem of space filling and bordering in a lively and pleasing, if restrained, manner. By the early nineteenth century, patterns like these had become part of an international vernacular, and their descendants are still famililar in wallpaper pattern books of our own day.

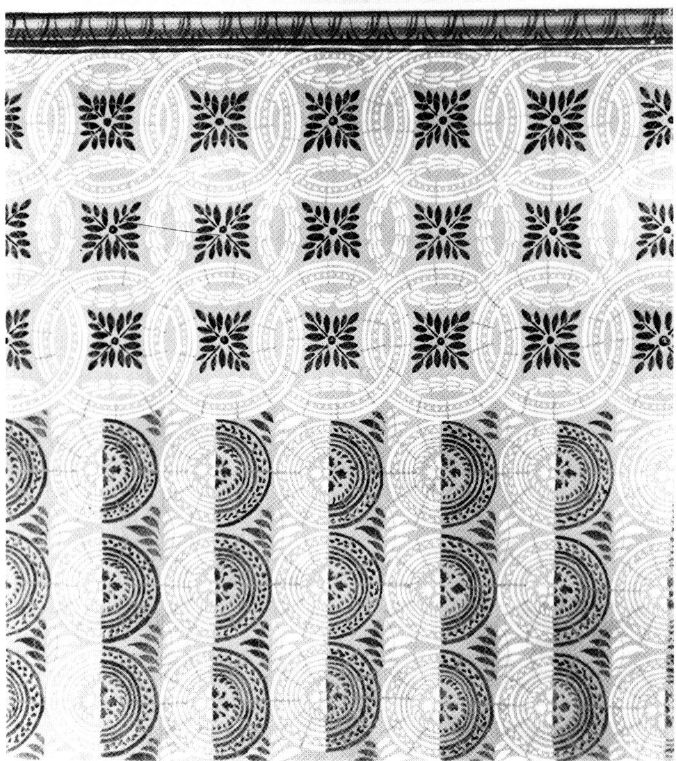

Figure 12
Three designs for wall patterning and border decorations, probably designs for stencilling, but closely related to and derived from wallpaper design. Each design shows two alternative wall patterns
Probably Austria, about 1820
Purchased in memory of Mary Hearn Greims, 1940-120-68, -9, -56

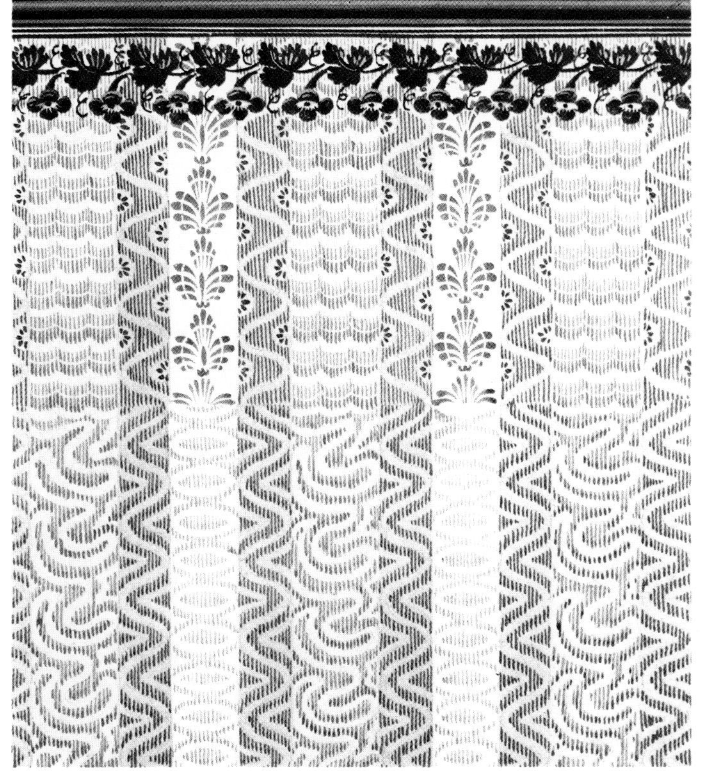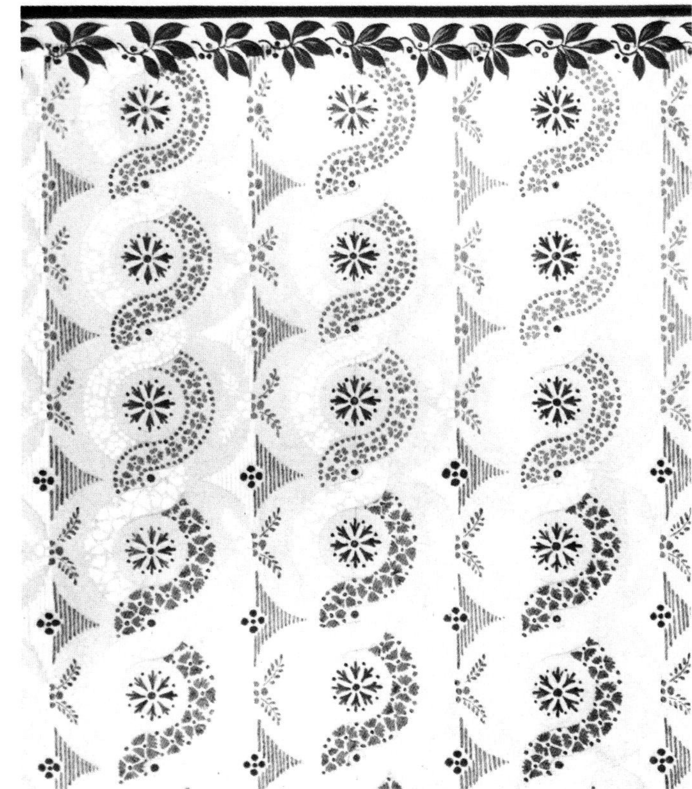

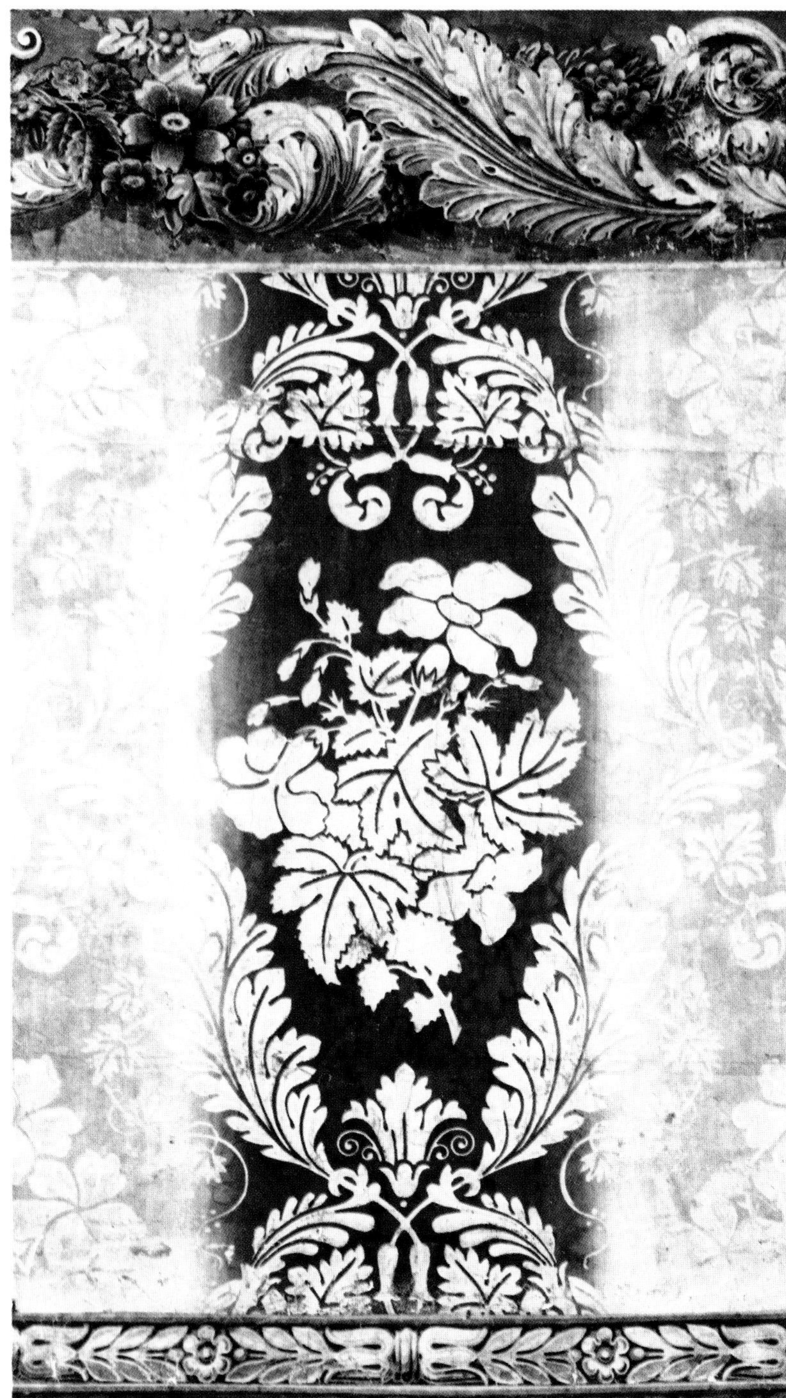

A great many patterns incorporating similar motifs were embellished with a coloring technique developed during the 1820s at the Zuber factory in Alsace. It was a technique for printing patterns and laying on ground colors in skillfully blended shadings from color to color, giving what Americans called a "rainbow" effect. The French called their color-blended patterns "irisé" or "ombré". To achieve the subtle color gradations in block-printed patterns, a range of colors was brushed onto a surface from which the wood block picked up the colors, that surface serving much as an ink pad does for a rubber stamp. The shifts through tones and hues of colors produced dramatic optical effects on walls. The color-shading created a tooled counterpoint to the shades in the patterns. In figure 13, a pattern in which a colorblended or *ombré* technique has been used for the background, is shown between two borders.

Wider friezes, narrower borders above chair rails, and still narrower edgings running vertically and over doors, mantles, windows, and other architectural features of a wall, were used in conjunction with a variety of wallpapers. The use of borders at cornice or frieze level was all but ubiquitous in late eighteenth and nineteenth century rooms.

More three-dimensional than the last examples, but seeming to exist within the confines of a shallow space that appeared to project slightly from the wall, were the countless realistic floral patterns produced during the middle years of the nineteenth century. French, English, German, and

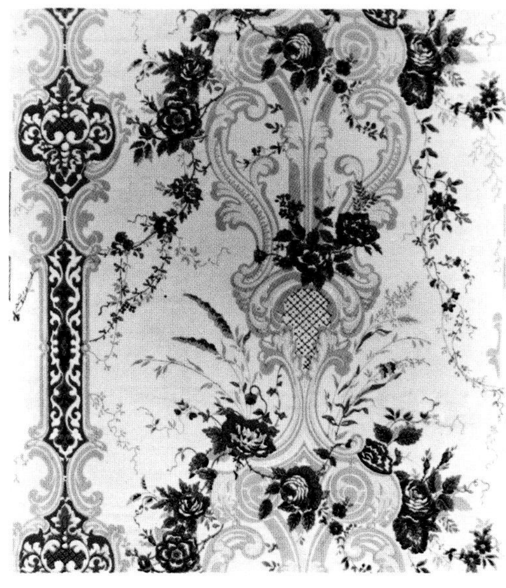

Figure 14
Floral striped wallpaper, block and machine printed
    on continuous, machine-made paper with a satin-
    finished ground
Probably France, possibly England, 1835-50
22 inches wide, bright blue, pink, orange and maroon
    flowers with bright green foliage, scrollwork in
    gray, blue, and gold on satin white ground
From the early-nineteenth century home of John Early,
    Lynchburg, Virginia
The gift of Mrs. John Early Jackson, 1969-144-1

American designers delighted in combining carefully shaded and intricately detailed flowers with scrolls — ornaments derived from baroque and rococo sources (Figure 14). Such designs often formed wide stripes when hung on a wall.

"Scrollwork" was a particular target of the derision of critics like Augustus Northmore Welby Pugin (1851 – 52), an architect and designer who scorned the visually illogical use of shaded forms that seemed to pierce and to project from walls. As he held up medieval architecture as the model for contemporary buildings, calling Gothic the "true Christian architecture", so he cited patterns of the Middle Ages as the best sources for wallpaper designs. In his own such designs for the Houses of Parliament, he adapted motifs from medieval wall paintings in which simple abstract forms were boldly outlined and filled with flat colors and arranged in regular repeats, creating a clear geometric order in the pattern (Figure 15).

Although Pugin and a number of other influential English critics and reformers of design pleaded for the adoption of such patterns, the commercial wallpaper industry apprehended the message that Gothic was good, but missed the point of just why the reformers thought so. English, French, and American wallpaper factories through the mid-nineteenth century produced thousands of "gothick" patterns like that of figure 16. Pugin would have viewed it as an illogical and trivializing reduction of architectural forms to inappropriate uses, piling arch over arch, pinnacle over pinnacle

Figure 15
Armorial wallpaper designed by A.W.N. Pugin (1812-
    1852) for the family of Washington Hibbert, Bilton
    Grange, Warwick
England, probably manufactured by William Woolams
    and Company for J.G. Crace (Stamped verso:
    CRACE: 14 WIGMORE STREET/11); 1841-1851
18½ inches wide; primary shades of blue, green and red
    with black outlines on white ground
The gift of Cole and Son, Ltd., 1953-134-1

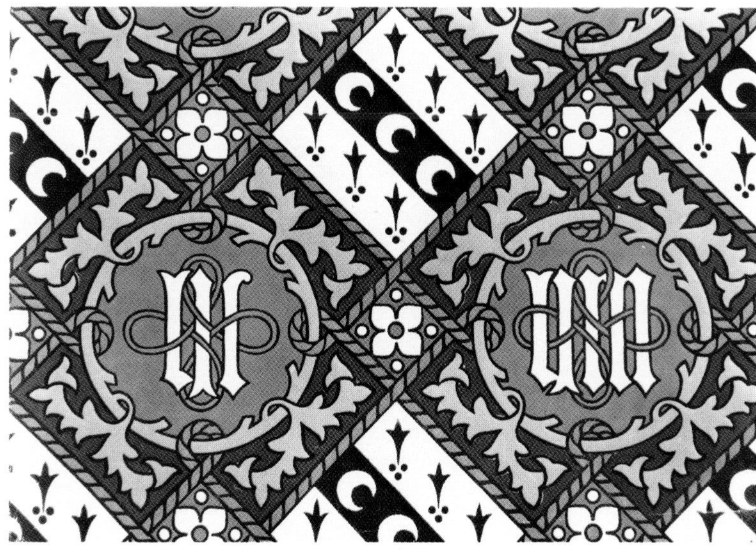

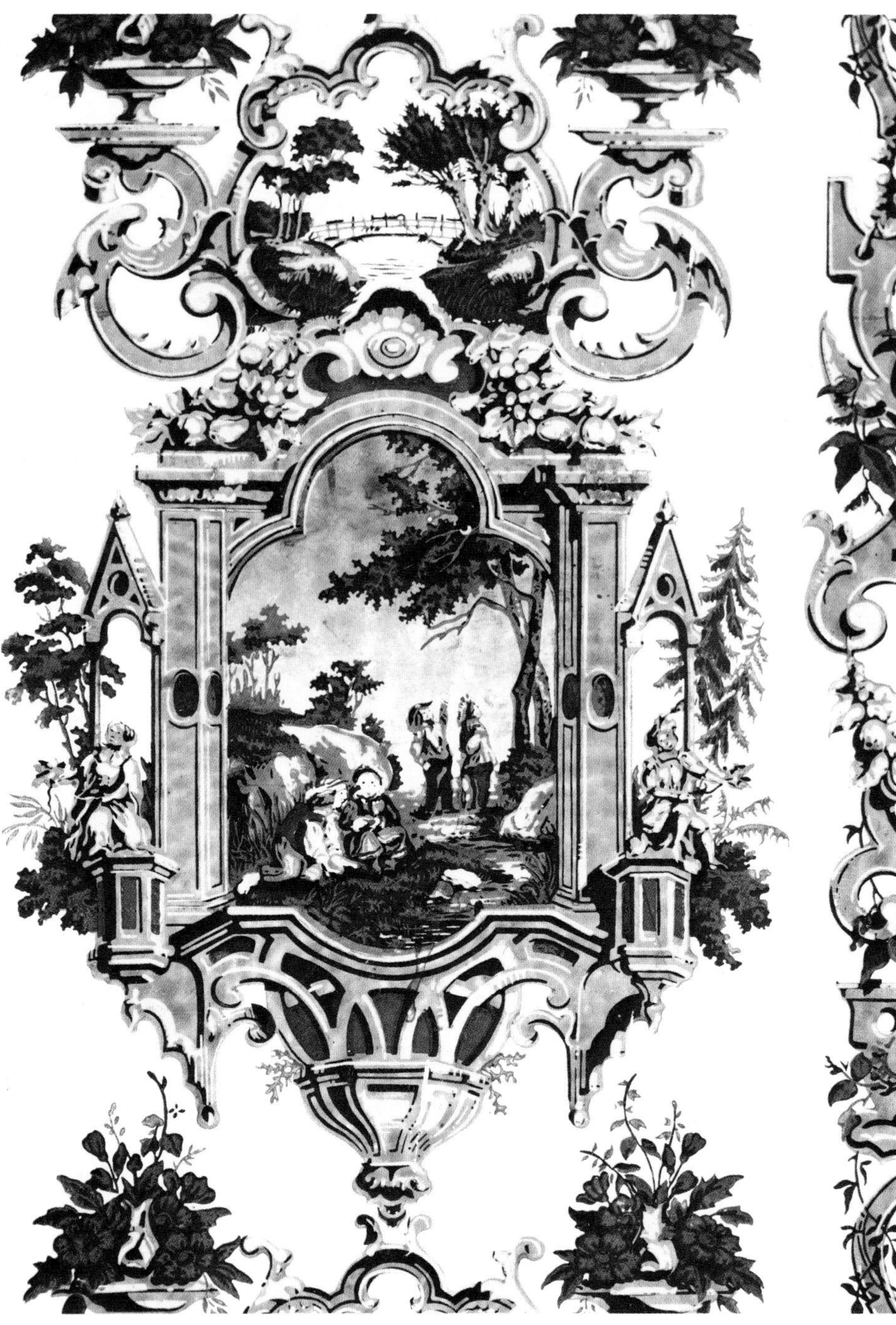

without end or reason, and in this case add-
ing some of the abhorred scrollwork, just to
cap its offenses. However, a great many
decorators of the period embraced similar
composite styles, to judge by the numbers
of patterns of this kind which survive.

By the mid-1830s, the means were
available for producing ever greater quantities of wallpaper by machine. Wallpaper
printing machines incorporated rollers
with raised printing surfaces, and were
adaptations of the machines developed for
printing textiles. Through the middle years
of the century they churned out thousands
of variations of patterns like figures 14 and
16 in a bewildering variety of styles.

Despite critical English pleas for sim-
plicity in wallpaper design and for the
use of two-dimensional patterns, Anglo-
American decorators continued to buy
elaborate French architectural fakery. The
pilaster shown in figure 17 is an element
from a *décor* — a set of decorations for a
room — that included a frieze or cornice and
a dado. In combination with pilasters they
would have been used to divide the walls
into panels. For the centers of some panels,
repeating patterns were chosen while in
others, flower-filled wallpaper urns or
statues were preferred.

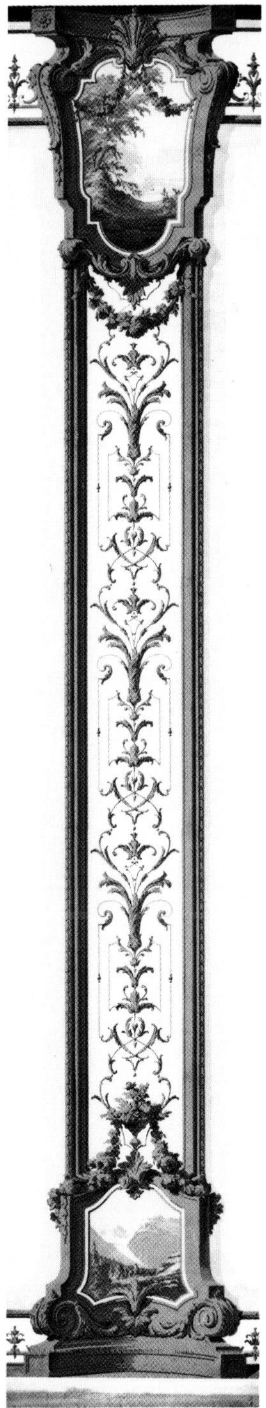

Figure 17

Wallpaper pilaster, an element from the panel set
  "Regence" which included dado and cornice
  elements, as well as centers for the panels formed
  by the elements imitating architectural details;
  block-printed in distemper colors on continuous,
  machine-made paper
Paris, printed by Jules Desfossé (1816-89) or by
  Desfossé et Karth (active 1842- 1930s); 1851-65
22 inches wide; shades of brown and gold on a gray
  ground, with the scenes in shades of blue, lavender,
  green and white
The gift of A. Germain, 1955-3-1

Window shades provided surfaces for
mid-nineteenth century wallpaper manu-
facturer's exercises in the arts of illusion.
Some depicted fake draperies — elaborate
imitations of velvet and damask curtains
over sheer white undercurtains, often com-
plete with lace, tassels and fringes. The
trade called these window shades "curtain
papers," although they rolled up as do
modern shades. The example shown as
figure 18 is the product of wallpaper printing machines. It commemorates an historic
event — New York's world's fair of 1853, a
celebration of the new industrial age. The
window shade shows the greenhouse-like
structure which was built on the site of the
present New York Public Library in imitation of London's Crystal Palace of 1851.

The New York Crystal Palace was a
showplace for American wallpapers, but
English and various European manufacturers were also represented there, and their
products were sold quite successfully in this
country. French papers continued to dominate international fashion, but during the
middle years of the century a group of
wallpapers imported from Germany enjoyed a vogue in this country, as well as in
France and England. They exploited techniques developed to emboss intricately

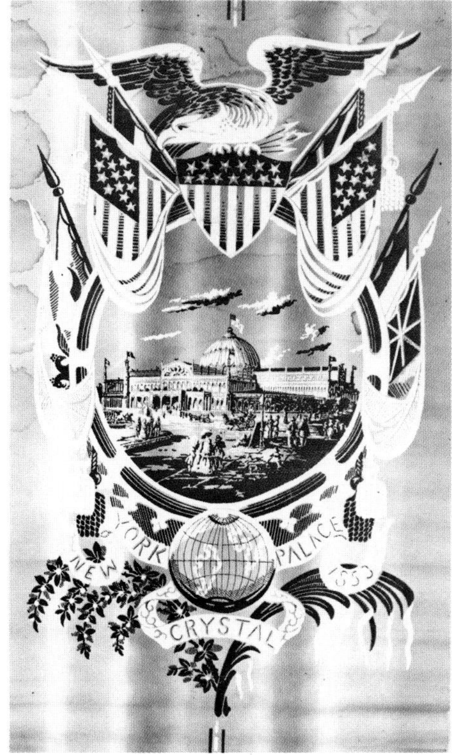

Figure 18

Window shade or "curtain paper" commemorating
  the New York Crystal Palace Exhibition of 1853;
  printed on wallpaper-printing machines on a single
  length of machine-made paper
United States; 1853
34½ inches wide; white and brown over a ground of
  colors blending in vertical stripes from blue on
  either side through gray and green to a central stripe
  of red
Purchased in memory of Eleanor and Sarah Hewitt,
  1944-66-1

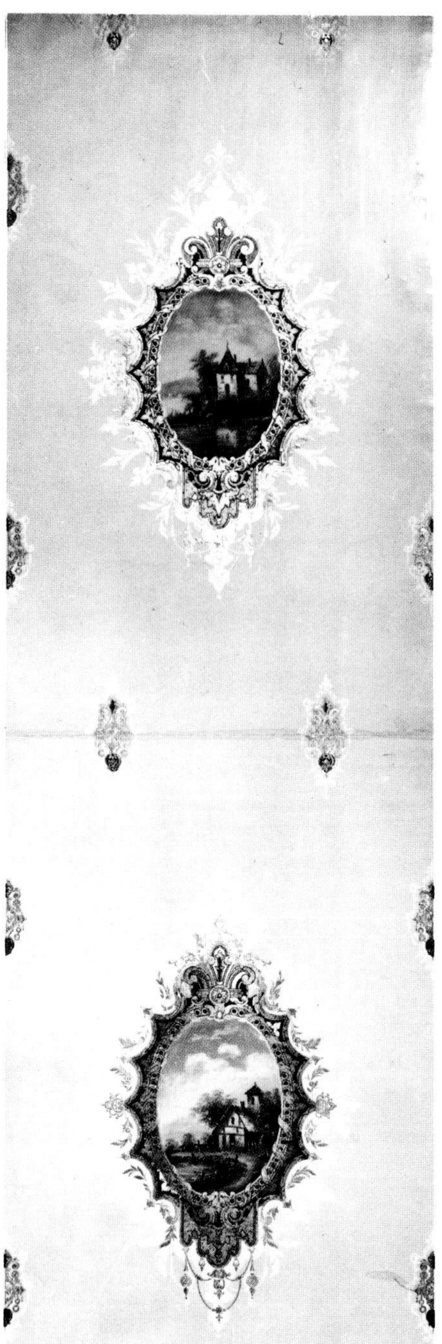

detailed motifs in 14 karat gold onto the wallpaper surface. These were soon being imitated internationally. In contrast to many densely-packed patterns of the period, the most popular among the German embossed gold papers featured relatively small-scale and isolated motifs, spotted over white or stone-colored grounds.

By the 1870s, English wallpapers were flooding the international market, in large part because of the popular success of designs by William Morris (Figure 20). His abstract and stylized motifs drawn from nature rendered his patterns flat enough to suit the English critics, while his naturalism attracted those who had always loved flowers on their walls. Morris had his first wallpapers printed in 1864. He was best-known among a number of English designers whose wallpapers finally outshone those of the French in the eyes of the fashionable.

Dr. Christopher Dresser, trained as a botanist, was nearly as well known as Morris for his wallpaper designs. While Morris, following Pugin's principles, valued hand-craftsmanship over machine production and preferred block printing to the new machine printing techniques,

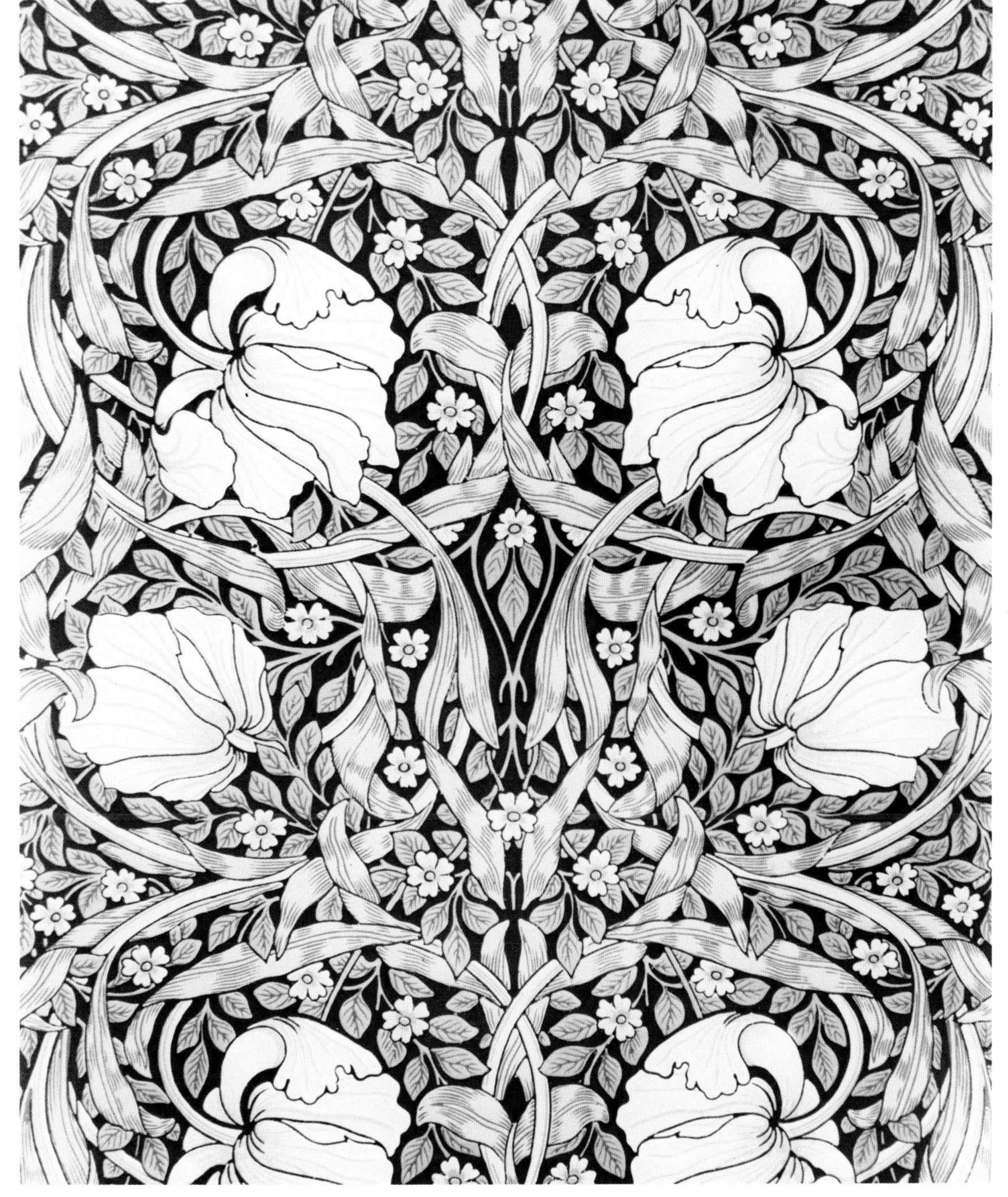

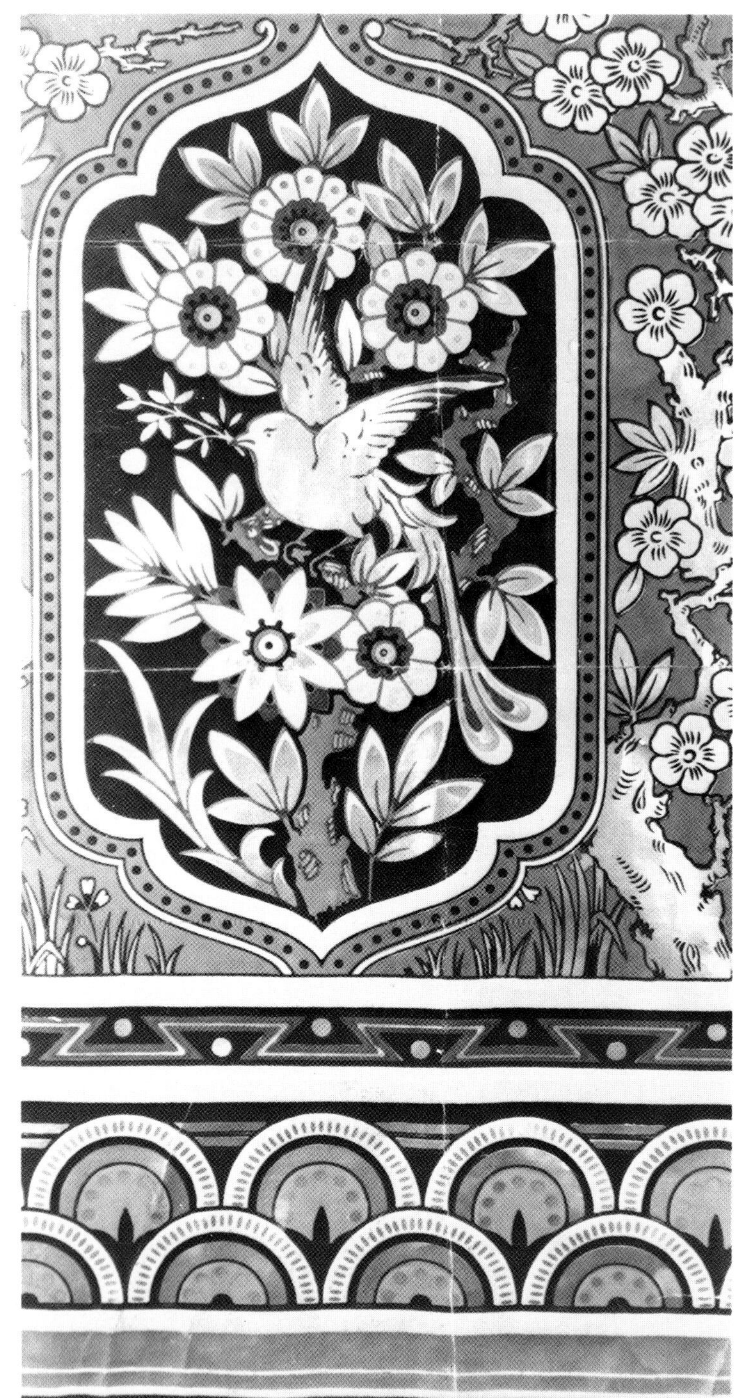

Dresser enthusiastically embraced the idea of designing for machines. He was, in fact, a pioneer in industrial design. Morris had looked to the middle ages for design inspiration, but Dresser and a number of other avante-garde designers in England turned to Japan (Figure 21). In the art of Japan, Dresser and his colleagues re-discovered abstract, two-dimensional forms, developed and refined through the centuries in both fine and decorative arts. Japanese patterned textiles were among the most important sources for stylish English wallpapers of the 1870s and 80s. The English popularized Japanese motifs for wallpapers, but gave them a distinctive touch which led American journalists to describe the style as "Anglo-Japanesque."

In Figure 22, another example of the Anglo-Japanesque is rendered in three-dimensional relief imitative of embossed leather, the material with which this brief overview began. Here a style created by designers preoccupied with the elimination of three-dimensional illusion is, ironically, rendered in three dimensions. The material is in fact neither leather nor paper, but a composition closely akin to linoleum, and

like linoleum, based on linseed oil. It was
called "Lincrusta," and advertised as "the
indestructible wallcovering". From the
time of its invention in England in 1877
until the 1920s it was one of the most popular wall coverings sold by wallpaper
dealers. Lincrusta had many competitors.
Some were, in fact, paper products.
"Japanese Leather Paper" was one of the
most widely distributed among them.
Made in Japan, it was usually gilded and
oiled as well as colored and embossed in
deceptively realistic imitation of leather.
Some examples looked like Spanish,
Flemish, or Italian examples of the seventeenth century; others were more purely
Japanese in design.

Designers of Art Nouveau patterns
carried into the twentieth century the
nineteenth-century concern to create non-
illusionistic two-dimensional patterns. For
the attenuated forms and agitated whip-
lash lines that characterize French and
Belgian Art Nouveau patterns, English designers like C. F. A. Voysey and his American imitators substituted more placid
curves, and fuller, broader forms (Figure
23). Such patterns, and many others pro-

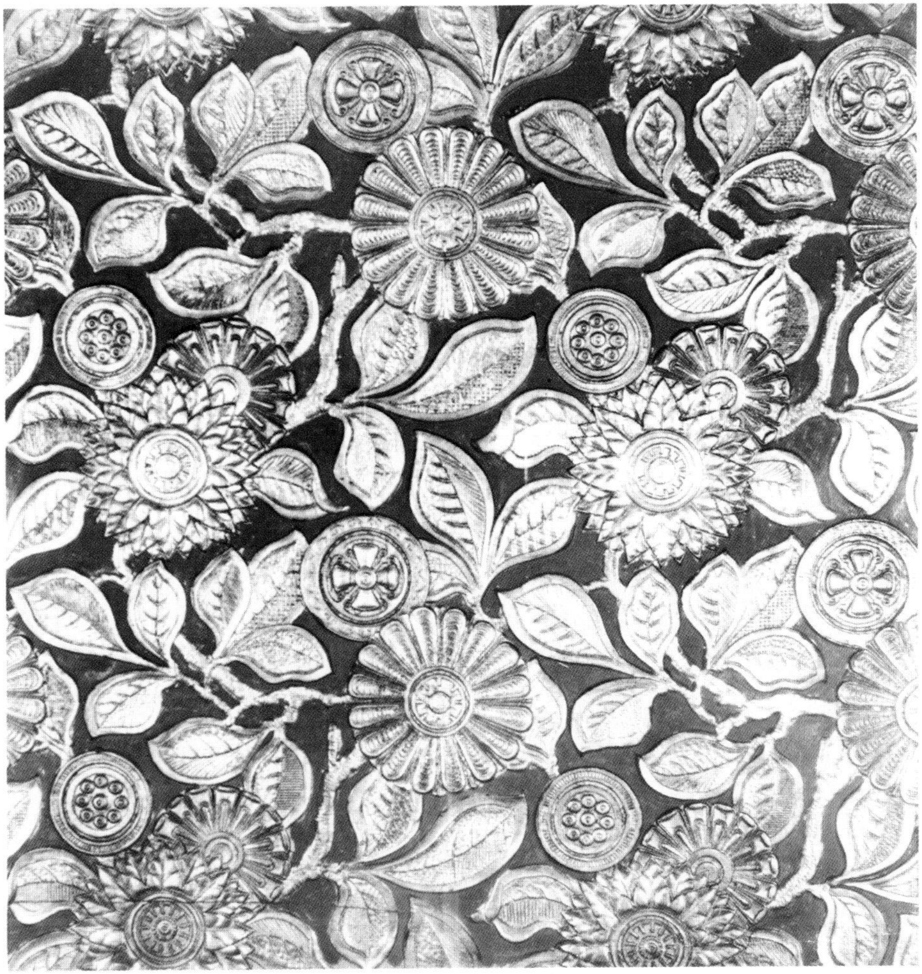

Figure 22
Lincrusta-Walton wallcovering with Anglo-Japanese
        patterning molded in relief
England; 1880-1890 in the style of Bruce Talbert
        (1838-81)
From the dining room of the John Davison Rockefeller
        House, 4 West 54th Street, New York
18½ inches wide; metallic gold on deep red ground
The gift of John Davison Rockefeller, Jr., 1937-57-3

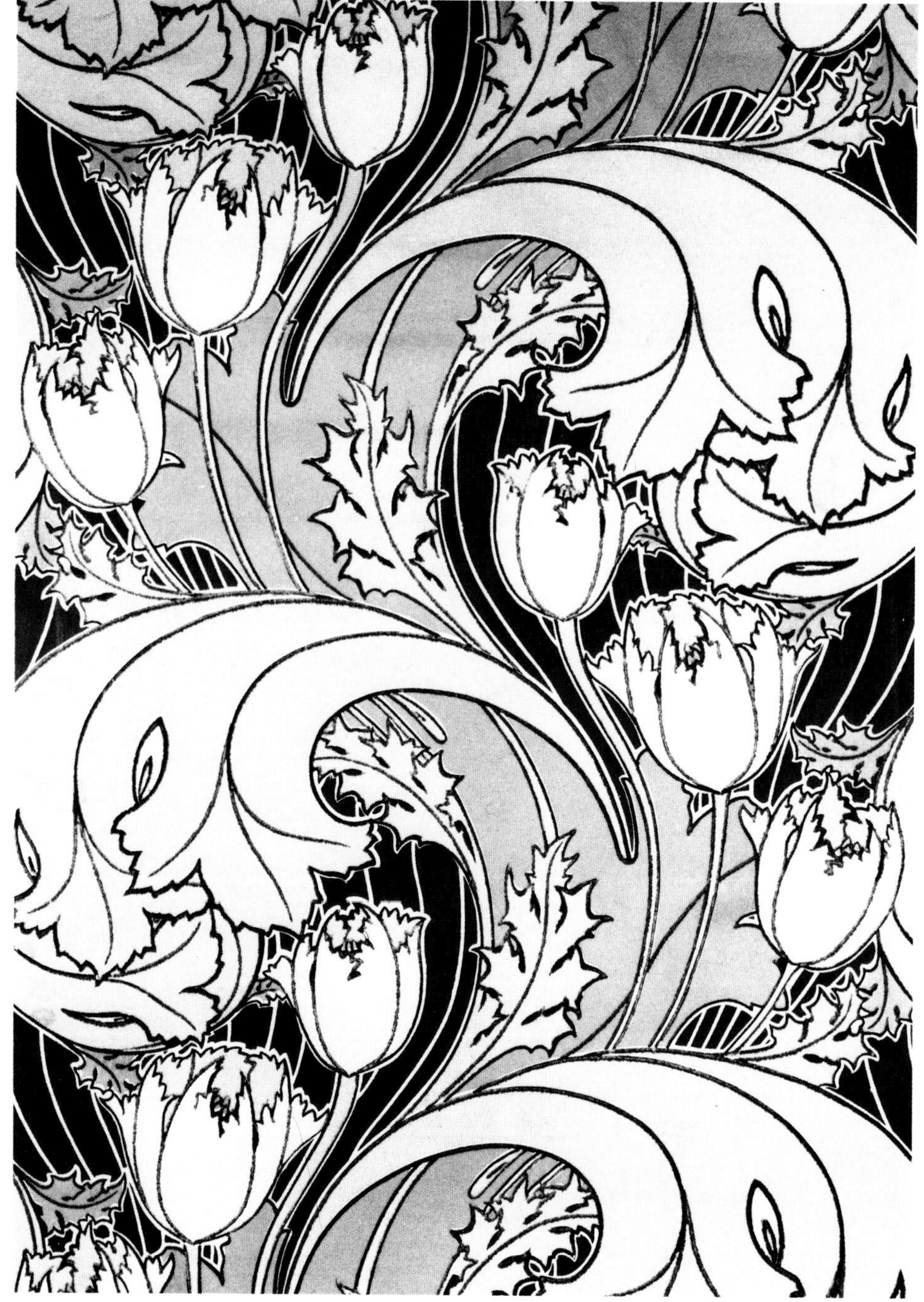

duced in England and America, owe a large debt to the floral and foliate patterning of William Morris, and to the patterns of another English designer of the late nineteenth century, Walter Crane, whose wallpapers are also represented in the Cooper-Hewitt collections. These designs are clearly related to the scrolls and curves of eighteenth-century rococo forms, yet equally evident is the concern of their designers to create an original, non-revival style.

Despite the Modernist's devotion to the white wall, some designers influenced by ideas of architectural Modernism felt a need for patterning appropriate to houses whose creation was dominated by functionalist concerns. Like the creators of Art Nouveau patterns, many of them, especially in Austria and Germany, continued to design according to some of the principles laid down by English theorists of the nineteenth century who demanded abstract, strictly two-dimensional, non-illusionistic (i.e. "honest") wallpaper patterns. And again like the creators of Art Nouveau designs, they strove for originality and inventiveness in their wallpapers. Figure 24

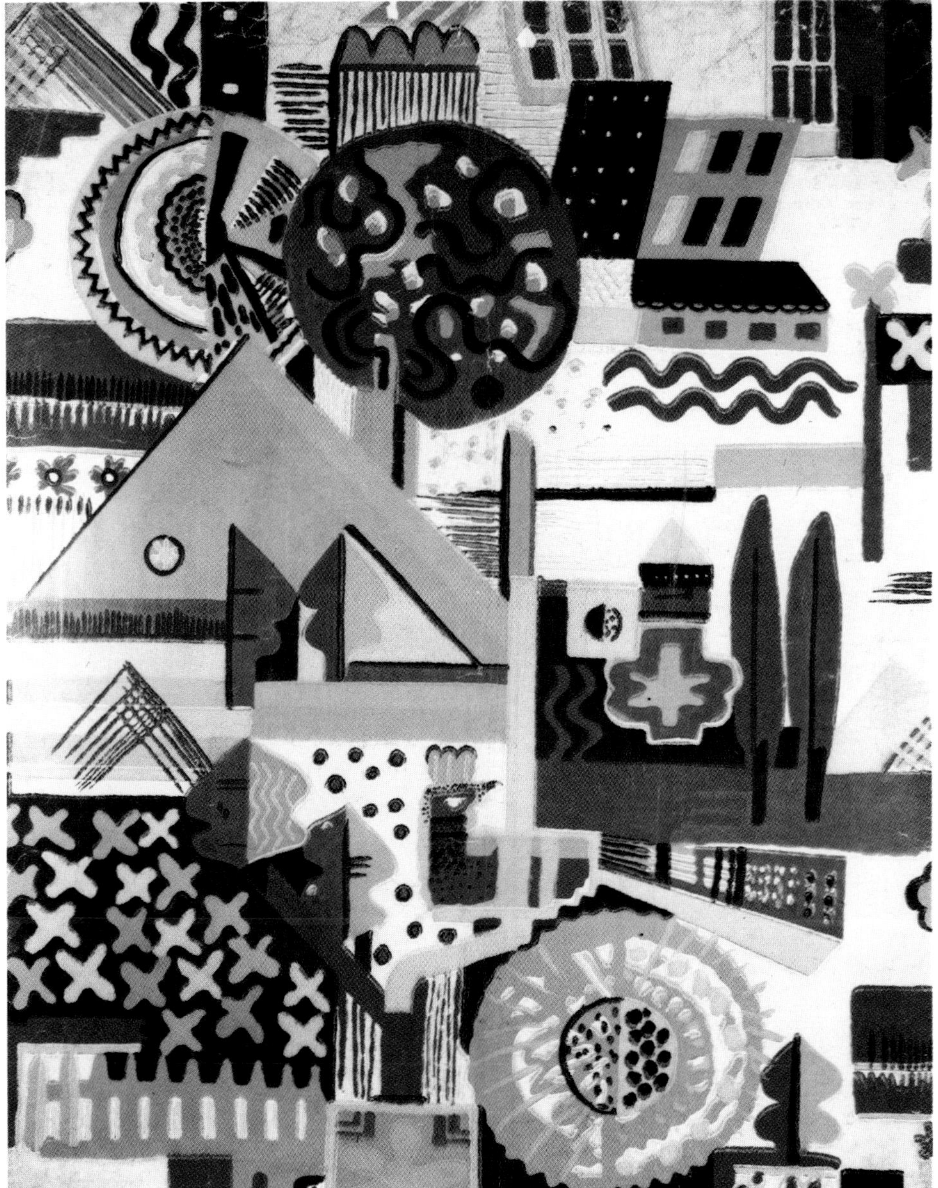

illustrates one among the many types of patterns that resulted from attempts to reconcile the sometimes contradictory demands of modernist theorists with the love of pattern and the tastes of the consuming public.

While many customers wanted something "modern" in wallpaper design, a great many others chose wallpaper patterns that were self-conscious revivals of earlier styles. Not only in America, with its Colonial Revival dating back as far as 1876, but also in Britain, France, and the other European countries, decorators created a steadily increasing market for a series of revival styles, including the neo-rococo, the Adamesque, and the neo-Renaissance. Wallpaper manufacturers recapitulated and adapted in new guises the succession of decorative styles surveyed here. The market for reproduction patterns has grown steadily since the 1920s, encouraged by the taste for Colonial Williamsburg's patterns, and for a succession of other museum recreations of early styles.

The Cooper-Hewitt continues to collect examples of historic as well as of contemporary wallpapers, attempting to

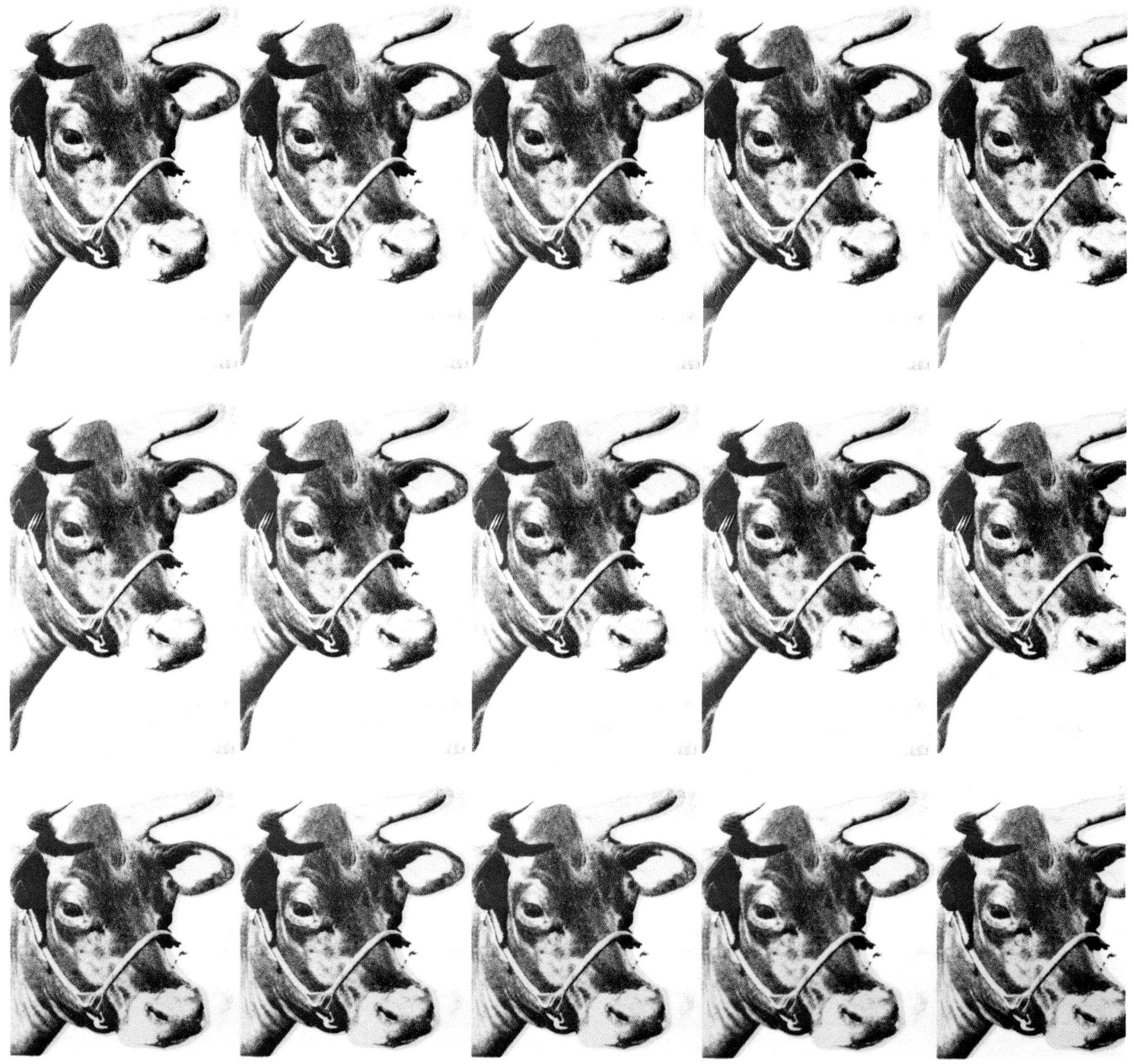

preserve fine examples representative both of relatively typical current decorating tastes as well as of the innovative and trend-setting. Among the many developments of recent years within the wallpaper industry, the use of new materials and techniques are striking. Metallic foils of the 1960s remind us of the beloved glimmers of gold dating back to seventeenth-century leathers. Refinements in technique include complex improvements of printing machines ranging from the use of photographically-generated aluminum rollers to computerized controls. In the part of the industry that caters to special orders and small-run, high-fashion designs, refinements in techniques for silk screen printing have marked recent years. The use of silk screens — very sophisticated stencils — on an appreciable scale in the wallpaper industry dates to the close of World War II.

Some of the most interesting stylistic developments in wallpaper design of recent years are closely intertwined with movements in the fine arts. Just as wallpaper manufacturers of the 1870s and 80s enlisted established artists to design wallpapers, a number of manufacturers have recently commissioned designs (Figure 25).

But in addition, the emergence of styles in painting and sculpture that are in themselves decorative and in some cases even wallpaper-inspired, have perhaps served to raise consciousness of the visual possibilities for covering walls with paper. Super graphics and pop art of the 1960s made many people look again at the wallpapers from which the paintings themselves appear to have derived a great deal, sometimes in terms of sheer wall-covering capacity, sometimes because the paintings were made up of repeating, patterned images. In the galleries, the presence of so many paintings that covered whole walls probably contributed to the rehabilitation of the status of wallpaper. And the tendency of many recent artists to enlarge scale, to blow up the insignificant and ordinary to a size that in itself lends monumentality to the lowliest of objects, has in turn suggested enlargement of scale in motifs printed on papers. The oversized cow-heads in Warhol's paper reflect this.

Looking again at Warhol's wallpaper cows suggests how strongly repeating images on wallpapers have influenced modern artists, not only Warhol with his rows of soup cans or Marilyn Monroe faces in paintings that pre-date the bovine wallpaper, but also artists whose importance has been as staggering as that of Picasso. Picasso's collages of the 'teens incorporate any number of actual samples of wallpaper, and his painted images for years thereafter include painted echoes of these patterns.

These instances reconfirm the power of wallpaper to contribute to and gain inspiration from the architect, the sculptor, and the painter, and attest to the intimate interconnections of wallpaper with the other decorative arts. Because early in this century the Hewitt sisters recognized the worth of wallpaper, even though it was not among the valuable "collectibles" eagerly sought and traded by stylish connoisseurs of their era, we now have at the Cooper-Hewitt Museum a major collection which many kinds of artists, students, and visitors may study and simply enjoy.

—*Catherine Lynn*

Short Selected Bibliography

Aslin, Elizabeth. *The Aesthetic Movement.* New York: Praeger, 1969.

Clark, Fiona. *William Morris: Wallpapers and Chintzes.* London: Academy, 1973.

Dornsife, Samuel A. "Wallpaper." *The Encyclopaedia of Victoriana,* edited by Harriet Bridgeman and Elizabeth Drury. New York: Macmillan, 1975.

Durant, Stuart. *Victorian Ornamental Design.* New York: St. Martin's Press, 1972.

Entwisle, Eric A. *The Book of Wallpaper.* London: Arthur Barker, 1954.

———. *French Scenic Wallpapers 1800–1860.* Leigh-on-Sea, England: F. Lewis, 1972.

———. *A Literary History of Wallpaper.* London: B. T. Batsford, 1960.

———. *Wallpapers of the Victorian Era.* Leigh-on-Sea, England: F. Lewis, 1964.

Frangiamore, Catherine Lynn. Wallpapers in Historic Preservation. Washington, D.C.: National Park Service, 1977.

———. "Wallpaper: Technological Innovation and Changes in Design and Use." *Technological Innovation and the Decorative Arts: Winterthur Conference Report, 1973,* pp. 277–305. Charlottesville, Va.: University Press of Virginia, 1974.

Greysmith, Brenda. *Wallpaper.* New York: Macmillan, 1976.

Hotchkiss, Horace. "Wallpapers Used In America, 1700–1850." *The Concise Encyclopedia of American Antiques.* 2 vols, edited by Helen Comstock. New York: Hawthorne Books, 1958. Vol. 2, pp. 488ff.

Justema, William. *Pattern: A Historical Panorama.* Boston: New York Graphic Society, 1976.

———. *The Pleasures of Pattern.* New York: Reinhold, 1968.

Lynn, Catherine. *Wallpaper in America.* New York: Cooper-Hewitt Museum and the Barra Foundation, 1981.

McClelland, Nancy V. *Historic Wall-Papers from Their Inception to the Introduction of Machinery.* Philadelphia and London: J.B. Lippincott Company, 1924.

Musée des Arts Décoratifs. *Trois Siècles de Papiers Peints.* Paris: Musée des Arts Décoratifs, 1967.

National Trust for Historic Preservation in the United States. *Documented Reproduction Fabrics and Wallpapers.* Washington, D.C.: National Trust, 1972.

Roth, Rodris. "Interior Decoration of City Houses in Baltimore: The Federal Period." *Winterthur Portfolio 5,* pp. 59–86. Charlottesville, Va.: The University Press of Virginia for the Henry Francis du Pont Winterthur Museum, 1969.

Sanborn, Kate. *Old Time Wall Papers.* Greenwich, Conn.: The Literary Collector Press, 1905.

Sugden, Alan V., and Edmondson, J.L. *A History of English Wallpaper, 1509–1914.* New York: Charles Scribner's Sons, 1925; London: B. T. Batsford, 1926.

Whitworth Art Gallery. *Historic Wallpapers in the Whitworth Art Gallery.* Manchester, England: The Whitworth Art Gallery, 1972.